'The Christmas story is God's way of telling us that we
are loved radically and unconditionally by him,
and this is how we are to be defined as people,
the people of God,
and the people who belong to God.'

TANYA
MAY GOD BLESS YOU
NOW AND ALWAYS
Duncan Song

This book is dedicated to my Mum, and the people of
Maigh Eo who in deeds, rather than words,
taught me all I ever needed to know about God.

All profits from the sale of this book are being donated to **The Society of Saint Vincent de Paul** based at Our Lady of the Wayside Catholic Church.

You can find out more about their work by going to:

svp.org.uk

and

ourladyofthewaysidechurchshirley.co.uk

# When Love Came Down

*Finding Christ in the Sunday Gospels of Advent and Christmas*

## Sean Loone

*Foreword by* **Father Andrew Franklin**

Michael Terence
Publishing

# Foreword

I first met the author of this book when I arrived at the Parish of Our Lady of the Wayside in Shirley in August 2020. One of the first presents I received upon arrival was a copy of Deacon Sean's latest book. What I then began to realise was that in Deacon Sean there is a wealth of scriptural and theological depth.

In the course of his ministry in the parish, Deacon Sean lives out that sense of diaconal service and charity. He regularly preaches God's word, celebrates baptisms, and comforts those who are bereaved. His homilies have added a pastoral depth that has benefitted the parish community. He also brings to his ministry the gift of teaching at Oscott and chaplaincy at Our Lady of the Wayside Primary School.

In this book Deacon Sean invites the reader to find Christ in the Sunday Gospels of Advent and Christmas. The readings throughout these two beautiful liturgical seasons are an invitation to draw closer to the joyful celebration of Christmas in an increasingly secular society. Deacon Sean journeys with us through the Gospels of Matthew, Mark, and Luke, ultimately helping us to journey towards our own salvation through the humanity of the newborn king.

In his writings Deacon Sean has sought to help spread the Gospel to the world at large, encouraging the reader to not only read about the faith but to go out, and live it as well, through practical language, and simple faith.

Having known and worked with Deacon Sean for some time now I have also realised that his work is never for personal promotion but a desire to live out the diaconate through service, charity, and love of neighbour. Over the years the profits from his work have gone to help numerous charities in their mission. The profits from this book will go to support the work of the Saint Vincent de Paul Society, a charity dear to my own heart.

I wholeheartedly recommend this book to you and pray that 'When Love Comes Down,' once again at Christmas, we will find Christ is at the centre of all that we say and do.

God bless you.

Fr Andrew Franklin<br>
Parish Priest<br>
Our Lady of the Wayside Catholic Church, Shirley

# Contents

# Introduction

When I sat down to write this book, I was uncertain as to what title to give it. To be honest, this is not unusual for me as I find that the title emerges, gradually, as I write. In the end, and after several failed attempts, I got to the point, whereby, the only title I could give to the project was, *'When Love Came Down.'* This is because, for me, such a title describes perfectly what happened at Christmas. If we believe that God is love and therefore the source of all love, and that Jesus Christ is His Son. Then Christmas is that moment, in time, when God sent his love to be with us so that we might know, and understand, what he is like.

This means that it is always God who takes the initiative. God who always comes in search of us. God who always makes the first move. God who comes to seek us out. God who always comes to find us. And why would God do this? Simply because he loves us. Through Jesus we are, in fact, overwhelmed by God's unconditional love. Yet, we can do nothing to deserve or earn such love because it is given to us, as a free gift. Something our modern minds find hard to comprehend. Unfortunately, the result of this can be, that we also find such love difficult to accept because it is just, too much. Hence, many people struggle to believe it, finding it easier to reduce the Christmas story to fantasy. Yet, Christmas, which belongs to everyone, is the story of radical, uncompromising love, which, perhaps, we are supposed to find difficult because it challenges, head on, our understanding not only of God, but also what it means to be a human being. In essence, the Christmas story tells us we belong to God, our Father, first.

What does this mean? The Christmas story is God's way of telling us that we are loved radically and unconditionally by him, and this is how we are to be defined as people, the people of God, and the people who belong to God. Such love by its very nature is intimate, revealed in the birth of a child who was born in a stable and laid in a manger, whilst at the same time sharing our flesh and blood. Why do we find this so difficult to believe? Perhaps, it is because that, deep down, we see ourselves as being unattractive and undesirable. Yet time and time again, throughout the Gospels, we discover a God who, through His Son, seeks out the rejected, despised, unwanted and unloved and assures them of one thing, his unconditional love.

Behind this way of understanding Christmas there is something very simple which we need to do if we are to grasp what God is about. This is to see ourselves, as being broken, and in need of healing. This, in fact, I would suggest is the first step to our awakening, a theme which reoccurs throughout the season of Advent, which is meant to prepare us for the momentous event to come. For to recognise that we are broken and in need of healing is to express our deepest desire, that of our need for God and his Grace.

In truth we are all lonely and in desperate need of understanding who we are. Perhaps, this is one of the reasons why there are so many mental health issues in society at the moment. So, what does God do? God sends His Son on a journey to penetrate the depths of our loneliness and to assure us of His love. Ultimately, only the love of God, revealed in His Son can truly set us free. All that God asks us to do in return, is to trust in that love and to abandon ourselves to it. Yet, to do this we have to let go of all those things which prevent us from recognising such love in the first place. One of the phrases I keep on using to describe this is, *God is closer to us than we could ever imagine and loves us more than we could ever know.*

What follows now is a journey through Advent into Christmas. My purpose is to invite the reader into this wonderful story of God's love, a love which comes in search of us, so that, hopefully, you will see it as your story too. Perhaps, now, you can begin to see and understand that there could, in fact, be no other title for this project other than, *'When love came down.'*

# Year A:

# Matthew

*'Behold, the virgin shall conceive and give birth to a son, and they shall call him Emmanuel, a name which means God-is-with-us.' (Matthew 1:23)*

# Matthew and Advent

We are about to embark on a journey with Matthew through the holy season of Advent. It is a time of preparation, of getting ready to celebrate the birth of Jesus at Christmas. So, what will Matthew have us do then? Firstly, we need to set aside some time, each week, to reflect on the Gospel reading placed before us, and secondly to think about its meaning for our lives of faith today. In summary, Matthew will invite us to do the following:

- To wake up, to be on the alert, to watch and to get ready for the coming of Jesus.

- To be ready to be converted and have a complete change of heart.

- To reflect on who Jesus really is and what this means for our lives of faith today.

- To understand the meaning of the name *'Jesus'* and why it is so fundamental to his mission.

Before we begin our reflections together, I would also say how important it is to recognise our need to be challenged in the way in which we live our lives of faith. Let us face it and be honest, Christmas comes, and Christmas goes and what changes? Very little! So, let this year be different and let us enter this holy season with open minds and soft hearts. Let us allow God through the grace of His Holy Spirit to speak to us directly, through the scriptures, as we prepare to celebrate the birth of His Son. Before we begin, however, let us pray that the coming of the Christ child, this Christmas, may so transform our lives that we become living flames of his love.

# One:

## 'Time to Wake Up'

Matthew 24:37-44

## First Sunday of Advent

*For as the days of Noah were, so will be the coming of the Son of Man. For as in those days before the flood they were eating and drinking, marrying, and giving in marriage, until the day Noah entered the ark, and they knew nothing until the flood came and swept them all away, so too will be the coming of the Son of Man. Then two will be in the field; one will be taken, and one will be left. Two women will be grinding meal together; one will be taken, and one will be left. Keep awake therefore, for you do not know on what day your Lord is coming. But understand this: if the owner of the house had known in what part of the night the thief was coming, he would have stayed awake and would not have let his house be broken into. Therefore, you also must be ready, for the Son of Man is coming at an unexpected hour.*

The words of Jesus, *'keep watch,'* made a deep impression on the early Christians, especially when they were linked to the end of the world. However, as this did not happen within their own lifetimes the words of Jesus needed to be understood in a different, though no less important, way. Jesus constantly made reference for the need to stay alert, be watchful and to stay awake but as time went by the early church spotted a problem. They were beginning to forget about Jesus and the power of his words, hence there was a real danger that when, in fact, he did return, he would find them asleep.

If we are totally honest with ourselves, we have the same problem today, do we not? Here on the first Sunday of Advent as we begin our preparations to celebrate the birth of Our Lord and Saviour Jesus Christ, we must be brave enough to ask ourselves the fundamental question, are we awake or have we fallen asleep? But what does this even mean? Think of it like this, is Jesus at the very centre of our lives? Does he give meaning, purpose, and value to everything that we do? Is Christ at the top of our list of priorities as we enter this holy season or have, we simply fallen into the trap of being consumed by the commercial world, which threatens to overwhelm us at this time of the year?

To answer these questions honestly and truthfully, we need to go back to Matthew's Gospel and reflect on what it means to *'keep watch.'* Here our focus needs to be totally and exclusively on Christ and our relationship with him. In what ways are we deeply attracted to Jesus? Can we live our lives without him? How is our faith in him reflected in the way in which we live? Have we, perhaps, fallen asleep, and in many ways deceived ourselves about our commitment to discipleship and the demands it makes on us? Can we identify the values of Jesus and honestly say that our lives conform to them? Have we fallen into the trap of going through the motions, observing the rituals of our faith but seeing no connection between how we worship and how we live? These, I know, are difficult and searching questions but Advent gives us the opportunity to literally *'wake up'* and reflect on what being a follower of Jesus today actually means.

Perhaps we need to be brave enough to admit that we need a new conversion, a fresh way of both seeing the world, and our faith with Christ, himself, at the centre. So, what do we do? Jesus, in fact, tells us, *'Wake up.'* The challenge is to look at our lives and the world around us with the eyes of faith and reflect on what happens next. The starting point must be with Jesus himself by knowing and believing that he is already at the core of our very being, closer to us than we could ever imagine, loving us more than we could ever know. Hopefully, this then gives rise to perceiving and understanding reality in a new way simply because we become more aware of what is actually going on around us. Hence, we can hear the voice of Christ himself in those who suffer, be more sensitive to his presence in our lives of faith and as a result become more tender and gentle-hearted towards each other; just like him. Such an awareness of his presence helps us to rediscover the footsteps of the Master who draws us ever closer to him, inviting us to serve and love others in the same way he serves and loves us.

It is essential in this process to be open to the challenges presented by the Gospel itself and not to turn away because the demands being made of us are just too great. Is it possible, therefore, that my own heart has, in fact, become like stone making me immune to the commandment to, *'love others in the same way I am also loved?'* Have I closed my ears to the demands made of me by Christ himself to be his disciple in the modern world? Are my eyes permanently shut as I refuse to look around me at others seeing them as Jesus did? If all or only some of this is true, have I, in fact, really fallen asleep only to find myself in the very trap my early brothers and sisters in Christ, all those centuries ago, tried so hard to avoid?

So, we come back to Advent and the start of a new liturgical year. Once again it is time to, *'wake up,' 'be on the alert'* and *'keep watch.'* The key is to stay close to Christ, to see through everything which the commercial world surrounds us with, and to simply be aware that he is already here knocking gently on the door of our hearts. Yet if we dare to open that door, he will challenge and make demands of us to live our lives in conformity with his. What does this mean? To see, hear and understand that Christ is, in fact, everywhere.

*Something to think about or discuss:*

1. *Spend some time, alone, with today's Gospel reading throughout the course of this week, seeing where and how it applies to your life of faith.*

2. *What do you think it means to have a heart of stone?*

3. *Reflect on how faith in Christ invites you to see, hear and understand the world differently.*

4. *Think about what Advent means to you and spend some time looking for signs of the season wherever you go.*

5. *Commit yourself to a short period of daily prayer reflecting on what it means to, 'keep watch'.*

**Two:**

## 'Time for Conversion'

Matthew 3:1-12

## Second Sunday of Advent

*In those days John the Baptist appeared in the wilderness of Judea, proclaiming, "Repent, for the kingdom of heaven has come near." This is the one of whom the prophet Isaiah spoke when he said, "The voice of one crying out in the wilderness: 'Prepare the way of the Lord, make his paths straight.'"*

*Now John wore clothing of camel's hair with a leather belt around his waist, and his food was locusts and wild honey. Then the people of Jerusalem and all Judea were going out to him, and all the region along the Jordan, and they were baptized by him in the river Jordan, confessing their sins.*

*But when he saw many Pharisees and Sadducees coming for baptism, he said to them, "You brood of vipers! Who warned you to flee from the wrath to come? Bear fruit worthy of repentance. Do not presume to say to yourselves, 'We have Abraham as our ancestor;' for I tell you, God is able from these stones to raise up children to Abraham. Even now the axe is lying at the root of the trees; every tree therefore that does not bear good fruit is cut down and thrown into the fire.*

*"I baptize you with water for repentance, but one who is more powerful than I is coming after me; I am not worthy to carry his sandals. He will baptize you with the Holy Spirit and fire. His winnowing fork is in his hand, and he will clear his threshing floor and will gather his wheat into the granary; but the chaff he will burn with unquenchable fire."*

As we reach the second Sunday of Advent it is time to think about something new and the need for our hearts to experience what can best be described as a conversion. But where do we start? Today's Gospel reading places us in the desert far from the Temple in Jerusalem and out of reach of Rome. It is here we come across the figure of John the Baptist and a man who knows he needs to spend time alone with God to prepare himself for what he must do next. Yet there is something different about this prophet which makes him stand out from all those who have come before him. He is not like the prophet Isaiah or any of the other prophets because he goes nowhere near the holy city of Jerusalem and the Temple. At the same time, he does not enter into debate or discussion with the religious leaders of the day, nor does he seek to clarify the Law of God for those who have gone astray. Equally he stays clear of all the well-known built-up areas of the region preferring the solitude and isolation of the desert. John knows all too well that he needs to spend as much time as he can in the presence of God, discerning and understanding exactly what he is called to be and do.

When we put all of this together, perhaps, we could best describe John as being independent. Or as a man and a prophet whose life is consumed by his love for God to the point that nothing else matters apart from doing his will. There can be little doubt that John had a deep and profound effect on the people who came to see him. The early Christians were absolutely convinced that John's primary task was to prepare the way for the coming of Jesus. What was it about John that drew so many people to him? Perhaps, it was the fact that he appeared to be a free spirit, controlled by nothing and no one, including the powers of Rome, the religious authorities or King Herod. The desert, of course, adds to this because it is a wild place, inhabited by few and controlled by nothing. It is here in this lonely and deserted place that John realises his mission and so becomes, *'A voice crying in the wilderness.'* Imagine, if you will, for one minute what the sight of John must have looked like as he emerged from the desert. He did not care how he looked or what people thought of him, rather he was a man on fire with love for God and he had a message to deliver.

Stop now for a moment and think about where you are in your journey through Advent. We have already reached the Second Sunday and Christmas draws ever nearer. The advertisements on television are in full swing, you may have already decorated your tree, the shops are bustling, and carols are in the air. Yet amongst all of this can you really hear the cry of John the Baptist? Going back to those early Christians, for them, John's primary role was to prepare the way for the coming of Jesus. As a result, in today's Gospel reading, we hear the words, *'Repent; prepare the way of the Lord, make straight his paths.'* But what does John mean by this and how can his desert cry impact on our lives of faith today?

Perhaps, we have to learn to hear John's words in a new way and be open to what the Holy Spirit might be saying to us afresh today. Key to this will be two things, our willingness to look at our faith in new ways and an attitude of conversion. The point has already been made that John's life was alive with God, you might say he was consumed and overwhelmed by a love beyond his ability to understand. Yet his mission was to prepare a way for another, who would be greater than him. John told the people straight that God was coming to them in a way he had never done so before but if they were to recognise him then they had to get ready and therefore undergo a conversion.

In this season of Advent, we too are invited to undergo a fresh conversion of faith. If we are to truly recognise and celebrate the birth of Jesus at Christmas and what this means for our salvation, then we must turn to Jesus now and undergo a conversion of our hearts. John's mission was not just to prepare the way for the coming of Jesus but to open up the path which led to him. For this reason, on this Second Sunday of Advent we need to really listen to John and focus our whole attention on Christ and what he means for us. That he, in fact, is the one who gives meaning, purpose and value to our lives and that we are loved unconditionally by him. Our hearts need to be set on fire by such love so that, like John, we are literally consumed by it. This is what I mean by conversion – a conversion of heart. It is not something that can happen overnight, but the key is to stay as close to Christ as possible and realise that our vocation, as his disciples, is to open the path to him for others. In this way, our hearts become like his because they have been set on fire by the flame of his unconditional love by which we, in turn, are overwhelmed. This is what I mean by something new, and this is what I mean by conversion. We know this is happening when compassion for others takes over our lives and we begin to see all people with the eyes of Christ himself. This then becomes not only our new way, but the new way of the Church and it takes us one step closer to celebrating our Saviour's birth. Now almost without knowing it, something has happened, something new, something different, something beyond our ability to understand or comprehend – our very lives have become conformed to that of Christ himself.

*Something to think about or discuss:*

    *1. How do you feel about spending time alone with God?*

    *2. What effect, if any, does John's message of repentance have on you?*

    *3. In what ways do you need to undergo a conversion of heart?*

    *4. Is it possible to think about our lives of faith in new ways?*

    *5. How might we open a path to lead others to Jesus?*

**Three:**

**'Who is Jesus?'**

Matthew 11:2-11

**Third Sunday of Advent**

*When John heard in prison what the Messiah was doing, he sent word by his disciples and said to him, "Are you the one who is to come, or are we to wait for another?" Jesus answered them, "Go and tell John what you hear and see: the blind receive their sight, the lame walk, the lepers are cleansed, the deaf hear, the dead are raised, and the poor have good news brought to them. And blessed is anyone who takes no offense at me."*

*As they went away, Jesus began to speak to the crowds about John: "What did you go out into the wilderness to look at? A reed shaken by the wind? What then did you go out to see? Someone dressed in soft robes? Look, those who wear soft robes are in royal palaces. What then did you go out to see? A prophet? Yes, I tell you, and more than a prophet. This is the one about whom it is written,*

*'See, I am sending my messenger ahead of you, who will prepare your way before you.'*

*Truly I tell you, among those born of women no one has arisen greater than John the Baptist; yet the least in the kingdom of heaven is greater than he.*

As we journey together through Advent the time has now come to reflect on who Jesus is and why he came? So, perhaps we could begin this reflection with a few questions before we explore the meaning of our Gospel passage for today.

1. Who is Jesus for you and how would you describe him?

2. Why do you think Jesus came?

3. What do you believe Jesus is calling you to do today as one of his disciples?

Give yourself the time and the space to reflect on your own answers to these questions and see what happens, especially as Christmas draws ever nearer.

Having explored John the Baptist's role in preparing the way for the coming of Jesus last time, we now find him imprisoned by King Herod. It seems, however, that John is now somewhat confused about who Jesus is. Perhaps, John like many of his contemporary Jews, was expecting a different kind of Messiah. One akin to his ancestor, King David, who would institute the judgement of God using force to defeat the power of Rome whilst at the same time saving all those who had accepted him by virtue of John's baptism in the river Jordan. What this tells us is that John was, in fact, confused about the identity of Jesus. Alone and imprisoned John's relationship with God and his understanding of the identity of Jesus was now the subject of confusion. He needed to know, for sure, that his mission had not been in vain and for that reason from the darkness of his cell he, somehow, managed to contact two of his own disciples and charged them with a task. They were to find Jesus and ask him a simple question, John wants to know, *'Are you the one who was to come, or should we expect someone else?'*

Such a question strikes at the very heart of the matter and would have also resonated with the early followers of Jesus. Indeed, it remains as relevant today as it ever was, hence our set of questions at the beginning of this reflection. There is a saying which goes, 'actions speak louder than words,' and this is exactly how Jesus answers the question presented to him. He does not send the disciples of John back with a clear-cut answer but rather invites the Baptist to answer the question for himself by reflecting on the deeds he has been doing, thus Jesus replies: *'Go back to John and report what you hear and see: the blind have their sight restored, the lame walk, lepers are cured, the deaf hear, the dead are raised, and the good news is preached to the poor.'* In other words, Jesus spells out quite clearly his healing mission and his calling to serve the despised, rejected, unwanted and unloved. Jesus associates himself, quite deliberately, with the marginalised of Galilee restoring their hope and trust in God. From this John is invited to draw his own conclusions as to the identity of Jesus. In many ways just as we saw on the first Sunday of Advent Jesus is, in himself, waking up the people as to the true nature and being of God.

So how can we 'know' Jesus today? Perhaps one of the best ways of doing this is, like John the Baptist, to reflect long and hard on what Jesus did and whom he spent most of his time with. In this passage on the second Sunday of Advent something is staring us in the face, it always has, but we have, if truth be told, been too blind to see it. If we are to truly 'know' Jesus, then we cannot afford to become too fixated on titles. Yes, Jesus is the Messiah and yes, Jesus is the Son of God but if we stay with these titles alone, we will never truly understand who Jesus really is. So, we need to ask, *'What does it mean to call Jesus the Messiah or the Son of God?'* But perhaps even more importantly than this we need to ask, *'What did it mean to Jesus?'* And this is where his answer to John the Baptist comes in because there can be no doubt, whatsoever, that Jesus associates his way of being the Messiah with relieving the pain, misery and suffering of humanity and offering *'good news'* to the poor.

In response to John's question Jesus, it would seem, is all too aware that there will be those both then and now who will be disappointed that he does not fulfil their expectations of being a judgemental and powerful Messiah. Indeed, this is how he puts it, *'Happy is he who will not feel let down by me.'* Equally, there is another message here and dare I say it a warning too, which is to avoid turning the Messiah into something we want him to be. You see the simple, yet profound truth is that God sent His Son and therefore His Messiah into the world for all people. His message is the Gospel of salvation for all. He includes everyone and excludes no one. It is so important that we embrace this truth if we are ever to really understand what the birth of Jesus means. He comes in search of us, he comes to find us, he comes to heal us, and he comes, ultimately, to lead us back to the Father of mercy, compassion, forgiveness, and love. And we see this clearly in the words of John the Baptist in today's Gospel reading.

Finally, then, how are we to respond to this as we take another step closer to celebrating Jesus's birth? If we are truly to commit our lives to Christ, then we must become like him so that others may experience him through us. We must associate our lives with what he committed his life to. So, to finish, imagine those outside the church or the Christian faith asking the same question John asked, but about us. When such people look at us, what do they see and what do they hear? Do they see and hear the words and the actions of Jesus, or do they see and hear something else? At Christmas we often pray that Jesus be born and live in us again. On this second Sunday in Advent, we are beginning to understand what such a prayer really means.

*Something to think about or discuss:*

    *1. How does Jesus live and speak in our lives of faith today?*

    *2. When people on the outside look at the church what do you think they see?*

    *3. Is it easier to believe in a judgemental and powerful Messiah?*

    *4. How does the Gospel reading help us prepare to celebrate the birth of Jesus?*

    *5. How do our lives and that of the church need to change to reflect more the teachings of Jesus?*

**Four:**

**'What's in a Name?'**

Matthew 1:18-24

**Fourth Sunday of Advent**

*Now the birth of Jesus the Messiah took place in this way. When his mother Mary had been engaged to Joseph, but before they lived together, she was found to be with child from the Holy Spirit. Her husband Joseph, being a righteous man and unwilling to expose her to public disgrace, planned to dismiss her quietly. But just when he had resolved to do this, an angel of the Lord appeared to him in a dream and said, "Joseph, son of David, do not be afraid to take Mary as your wife, for the child conceived in her is from the Holy Spirit. She will bear a son, and you are to name him Jesus, for he will save his people from their sins." All this took place to fulfil what had been spoken by the Lord through the prophet: "Look, the virgin shall conceive and bear a son, and they shall name him Emmanuel," which means, "God is with us." When Joseph awoke from sleep, he did as the angel of the Lord commanded him; he took her as his wife.*

As we arrive at the fourth Sunday of Advent and with Christmas, literally, just around the corner, I would like to invite you to do something. Spend some time reflecting on what it means to refer to Jesus as our *saviour*. Just give it some careful thought, discuss it with others if you can and then finally write something down so that you can compare what I am going to say with your own initial ideas.

Today's reading is in fact radical, now let us discover why. The angel tells Joseph in a dream that what Mary has told him is true. She is to give birth to a son, which she has conceived through the Holy Spirit, and he is to call the child Jesus, *'because he will save his people from their sins.'* The name Jesus actually means, *God saves* and here the angel makes it clear that this means *to save his people from sin*. In the ancient world, tradition dictated that the first-born son was named after his father but this child right from the beginning was to be different. His name would reveal his mission and his life would not conform to any human conventions.

Taking this point, a little further, it is important to appreciate that in the ancient world names were given for a specific purpose which was to establish identity, and therefore what the named individual was called to be and do. For the most part this involved loyalty to a tribe or clan and brought with it rights and responsibilities. In relation to Jesus and his name what we can see clearly here, therefore, is a revelation of his mission to the world even before he is born because *'he will save his people from their sins.'*

Yet the world at the time had another saviour and his name was Vespasian the new emperor of Rome. On entering the city having quashed a rebellion by the Jews he is heralded as the saviour of Rome and represents the mightiest empire the world has ever known. His strength and power are to be found in his legions, his wealth and riches are untold, indeed there are many who even regard him as a god.

So, against this background Matthew offers the world a different kind of *saviour*, one who will bring salvation not through might and power or war and tyranny but through mercy, compassion, forgiveness, and love. The world does need saving but from evil, injustice and oppression or putting it another way, from sin. In this way Matthew makes something abundantly clear that the world needs Jesus not Vespasian.

Now for another surprise and another name, did you spot it? *'The virgin is with child and will give birth to a son and they will call him Emmanuel – which means, God is with us.'* I cannot tell you how shocking this is. At one level we have an earthly name – Jesus, but now we also have another name – Emmanuel, which literally means, *'God-is-with-us.'* Here we have then, right at the start of Matthew's Gospel and before Jesus is even born, a clear declaration that he is, in fact, God and that he will be-with-us. And what will he do? He will save us. What from? Sin.

In his letter to the Philippians Saint Paul tells us, *'At the name of Jesus every knee should bend,'* (Philippians 2:10) and this gives us an insight into how early Christians revered the name of Jesus. In this way and indeed for Matthew the name Jesus gives expression to the Christian faith, and it is in his name that we live, move, and breathe. Thus, to utter the name Jesus is to confirm our belief that he is the source of our salvation, saving and therefore rescuing us from sin. And that is why the name of Jesus is so important.

I wonder though if we have not lost reverence for the name of Jesus treating it in an almost flippant way. Perhaps then, the time has come to rediscover something which we have always had, the truth that *God-is-with-us*. Advent gives us the opportunity to return to the name Jesus treating it with love and affection, recognising that all our hope rests in him who rescues us from sin and death. On this fourth Sunday of Advent then, let us call to mind what it means to whisper quietly and with great reverence the name Jesus, and let us never tire of having his name on our lips.

*Something to think about or discuss:*

1. *What do you think about the name Jesus now?*

2. *Do you think the importance of the name Jesus has been lost?*

3. *How can the name of Jesus be revered today?*

4. *Have we lost a sense of sin and what does this mean for our lives of faith today?*

5. *How does this reflection help us prepare to celebrate Christmas more effectively?*

# Matthew and Christmas

The first thing to note is that not all the readings in this Christmas season come, in fact, from Matthew. This is because the presentation of the unfolding story of Our Lord's early life needs to be read in such a way that it makes a deep impression on our hearts. The composition of the lectionary, therefore, takes a number of factors into consideration as the church reflects on the enormity of the incarnation and what it means for our lives of faith today. It is for this reason that the Gospel of Luke is used to complement that of Matthew in this most holy of seasons.

What better place to begin than with those shepherds on the hillside? Just another ordinary night like any other, until surrounded by the heavenly host their lives and that of the world are changed forever. Quickly they are told not to be afraid before everything changes again and the Holy Family are visited by a group of mysterious strangers from the East. Warned in a dream of the imminent danger posed by King Herod, Mary, and Joseph, frightened for the life of their child, find themselves on the run seeking refuge in a foreign land.

At this point, perhaps, we all need to stop just to take our breath and like Mary, *'ponder all these things in our hearts.'* After all, we are familiar with the story but what does it mean for our lives of faith today. The birth of the Christ child changes everything but what about our own hardened hearts? In what ways do we have to change, and in what ways do our lives need to be transformed if Jesus is to be born, anew, in us again? For this reason, giving ourselves time to reflect on these momentous events is essential, especially as we prepare to start a new year.

I often think about what happened to those Magi after they left that stable. We assume, of course, that they made their way home by a different route but what difference did their encounter with the Christ child make in the way in which they lived? After all, they had been preparing, their whole lives, to meet the King of Kings and Lord of Lords. It is something, however, we will never know the answer to, but we do have our own lives and, perhaps, this is where our attention needs to be focused. Is Christ the centre of our being, and does he give meaning to our lives here and now? Searching questions but is this the key to seeing the Epiphany in a different light, that we must never give up the search, no matter how long it takes, until that moment when we discover that it is he, in fact, who has already come and found us.

Finally, we come to Jesus standing on the banks of the river Jordan waiting to be baptised by John. In that moment, the *'Spirit of God'* descends on him, and he is identified by the Father as the Son. It is this same *'Spirit,'* which is poured into our lives, and it is this same *'Spirit,'* which draws us to Jesus. Let us, therefore, now make ourselves open to the *'Spirit'* as we prepare to reflect on the word of God together in this most holy of seasons. Yet, let us also never forget that the *'Spirit,'* changes and transforms us drawing us ever deeper into the life of God, awakening within us a treasure beyond price, faith.

**Five:**

## 'The Real Meaning of Christmas'

Luke 2:1-14

## The Nativity

*In those days, a decree went out from Emperor Augustus that all the world should be registered. This was the first registration and was taken while Quirinius was governor of Syria. All went to their own towns to be registered. Joseph also went from the town of Nazareth in Galilee to Judea, to the city of David called Bethlehem, because he was descended from the house and family of David. He went to be registered with Mary, to whom he was engaged and who was expecting a child. While they were there, the time came for her to deliver her child. And she gave birth to her firstborn son and wrapped him in bands of cloth, and laid him in a manger, because there was no place for them in the inn.*

*In that region there were shepherds living in the fields, keeping watch over their flock by night. Then an angel of the Lord stood before them, and the glory of the Lord shone around them, and they were terrified. But the angel said to them, "Do not be afraid; for see I am bringing you good news of great joy for all the people: to you is born this day in the city of David a Saviour, who is the Messiah, the Lord. This will be a sign for you: you will find a child wrapped in bands of cloth and lying in a manger." And suddenly there was with the angel a multitude of the heavenly host, praising God and saying, "Glory to God in the highest heaven, and on earth peace among those whom he favours!"*

If someone were to ask you, what is the real meaning of Christmas, what would you say? Give it some thought and if you must write your answer down before discussing and sharing it with others. Now ask yourself, what real difference does the celebration of Christmas make to your life? After all, we have just reflected together on the meaning of Advent and now the great day has arrived but what has really changed? I think we all know that many people celebrate Christmas, but do they know why? Equally we are all encouraged to pursue happiness but how long does it last? Perhaps, part of the problem is that we think we are all so familiar with the story of Jesus's birth that we have stopped listening to it. This year then let us go back to the biblical text itself, reading it prayerfully, carefully, and thoughtfully before then going on to reflect on what it really means for our lives of faith today.

Imagine the scene, a group of shepherds are out on the hillside doing what they normally do by tending to the needs of their sheep. The night is dark and cold and perhaps the shepherds are engaged in conversation about their plans for the day to come. In other words, for them it is a perfectly normal night, nothing stands out and, in the darkness, there is always, of course, the threat of wild predatory animals. Then all of sudden everything changes as they are literally engulfed by a glowing white light, referred to in the text as *'the glory of the Lord.'* It is not surprising, therefore, that the shepherds are terrified by what they see. I wonder were those shepherds comfortable in the darkness somehow comforted by the normality of their lives. If so, do we fall into the same trap? Are we so comfortable with the Nativity story, that it fails to shock us and therefore it has little or no impact on our lives of faith anymore? It is easy to miss the fact that the shepherds were not frightened by the darkness but by the light. It seemed to come out of nowhere and shattered their ordinary and everyday lives with its brightness because they did not expect it. We on the other hand, do expect it and so its impact on our lives is diminished but is that because we really fail to read the text? Or are we not open enough to the way in which the light of God can shatter the darkness of our own lives? Either way listen to the words of the angel, *'Do not be afraid.'*

Are we really afraid to let the light of God into our lives for fear of what it might do? Are we, therefore, more comfortable with staying in the darkness, where our lives of faith will never be challenged? Is this the key to understanding the real meaning of Christmas then; that we must be open to the light and the truth which it brings? Here then is our starting point by linking light with truth and allowing God to be God. Only by doing this can we begin to understand the real meaning of Christmas and the challenges its celebration must bring to our lives of faith today.

Now we need to reflect on what the angel says next but before we do that have you ever thought about what the difference is between joy and happiness? The world speaks a lot about happiness and our need to pursue it, but it rarely talks about joy, why is that? Very often we connect happiness with what might be called a sort of 'feel-good factor' which in turn gives rise to personal enjoyment or self-satisfaction, but this has the effect of making happiness all about me. So, now let us go back to the biblical text and see what the angel says to the shepherds, *'I bring you news of great joy that will be for all people.'* Straight away several important points need to be made about what all of this means for us and our lives of faith today. Firstly, the joy which is announced is unique and quite different from what we might call happiness, because it is *'great joy'* and reflects the *'good news'* which can only come from God through the announcement to the world of the birth of his Son, Jesus Christ. Secondly, and as a direct result of this announcement, such *'good news'* is *'for all people'* but especially for all those who feel that they have been rejected, despised, unwanted or unloved.

The important point to make here is that the coming of Jesus must be *'good news'* for us and his gospel must impact directly on our lives now. Not yesterday, not tomorrow but now and this must be received with *'great joy.'* You see the kind of *'joy'* we are talking about here is something which only God can bring, and it speaks directly to our hearts. As such, it is an invitation to confront all those negative connotations, we associated with happiness earlier. Such *'joy'* which comes only from God is nothing to do with selfishness, self-satisfaction or even well-being. It is nothing to do with feeling comfortable in our faith or the way in which we practice our religion and finally it is nothing to do with the way in which the secular world celebrates Christmas.

So, what is it to do with then? Well, once again, let us return to the biblical text and let the angel tell us through the words, *'Today a saviour has been born to you.'* And here it is, the *'good news'* for the whole of humanity, that the child to be born is for all of us. This Christ Child is to be nothing less than the *'saviour'* of the whole world and it is in him that we are invited to place all our trust and all our hope. In these words, from the biblical text, therefore, we have the final hope for the human race. Through him, finally, that which humanity has consistently failed to do will now be put right. In the birth of this child the world will be confronted with the reality of God. His love, his justice, his peace, his forgiveness, his mercy, and his compassion will burst through into our lives and invite us to place all our hope and all our trust in him. And here we discover the real meaning of Christmas, which is not to be found, ultimately, in making us feel comfortable and happy in the confinement of our own lives and in in our own homes as the world so often wants us to. But rather in the new hope for humanity offered to us by God through the birth of his Son, Jesus.

*Something to think about or discuss:*

1. *What would you say is the real meaning of Christmas?*

2. *How does the celebration of Christmas impact on our lives of faith today?*

3. *What do we need to change to make the celebration of Christmas more effective?*

4. *Why does the angel refer to Jesus as, 'saviour?'*

5. *Can you think of practical ways to encourage Christians to spend more time with the Bible?*

# Six:

## 'A Refugee and Asylum Seeker'

Matthew 2:13-15, 19-23

## The Holy Family

*Now after they had left, an angel of the Lord appeared to Joseph in a dream and said, "Get up, take the child and his mother, and flee to Egypt, and remain there until I tell you; for Herod is about to search for the child, to destroy him." Then Joseph got up, took the child and his mother by night, and went to Egypt, and remained there until the death of Herod. This was to fulfil what had been spoken by the Lord through the prophet, "Out of Egypt I have called my son."*

*When Herod died, an angel of the Lord suddenly appeared in a dream to Joseph in Egypt and said, "Get up, take the child and his mother, and go to the land of Israel, for those who were seeking the child's life are dead." Then Joseph got up, took the child and his mother, and went to the land of Israel. But when he heard that Archelaus was ruling over Judea in place of his father Herod, he was afraid to go there. And after being warned in a dream, he went away to the district of Galilee. There he made his home in a town called Nazareth, so that what had been spoken through the prophets might be fulfilled, "He will be called a Nazorean."*

One of the things we must constantly guard against when it comes to the Christmas story is the tendency to romanticise and fantasise it. This, of course, is something which the secular world encourages but it is not true to the Gospel of Jesus Christ, and the celebration of the Holy Family proves it. Thus, the world draws our attention first to Bethlehem flooding us with images of lambs, straw, and lanterns before idealising the life of the Holy Family as they settled down in the village of Nazareth nestled in the hill country of Galilee. The reality, however, is far from this distorted view of an idealised and therefore corrupted truth.

Matthew tells us plainly that right from the beginning the Holy Family were under threat from King Herod who would not tolerate any form of competition to his monarchy. Hence all boys under the age of two who lived in the vicinity of Bethlehem were to be put to the sword. As a result, there is no time to lose, and Joseph is warned in a dream to take his family and flee. Indeed, such is the danger that this must be done straight away, *'at night,'* and the destination is *'Egypt.'*

Such a journey with Joseph constantly looking over his shoulder would have been long, hard, and dangerous. As I write this, I cannot help but wonder did Joseph and Mary recall the journey their ancestors made through the wilderness all those centuries before? After all, it is, of course, the same desert. Were they conscious that in many ways they were, in fact, reliving the experiences of their own people, something Jesus was to continue to do throughout the Gospel of Matthew? In addition to this, not only were they refugees escaping a real threat to the life of their son, but they were also asylum seekers looking for sanctuary in a foreign land far from their home, their family, and their own people. The only thing the Holy Family could do now was place all their hope and all their trust in God despite being confronted with insecurity and uncertainty. Indeed, when all was said and done, they did not know, at least at this stage, whether they would ever see their homeland again. As a result, all they could do, was wait. This paints for us a far different scene from the cosy and comfortable image of Christmas we all grew up with and which, for the most part, is still portrayed today. Yet Matthew confronts us with a startling truth, that God did not spare his own son from the plight of suffering humanity. Indeed, the Gospel immerses Christ in the depths of human misery offering the hand of God to all those who suffer but especially here and at this point, the refugee, and the asylum seeker.

Once Herod has died there is a sense that the danger has now passed until we learn that Archelaus, his son, now reigns in Judea. History teaches us that he quickly develops a reputation for cruelty which threatens to surpass even that of his father. It is understandable, therefore, that we are told, Joseph *'is afraid.'* Hence, the Holy Family are on the move again, this time they make for Galilee where the land is rich, green, and fertile. They find a small village in the foothills called Nazareth where at last, they can settle down and build a home together. At this point, I find myself asking, was Joseph now relieved, did he feel that his family were now safe and that he could, at last, stop constantly looking over his shoulder, at least for a while?

It is a remarkable story of bravery and courage in the face of adversity. Once again, I find myself admiring both Joseph and Mary for what they were prepared to do to protect the life of their son. Moving from place to place, finding work wherever they could, whilst at the same time living constantly under the treat that Herod was still looking for them. In this way God identifies himself with all refugees and asylum seekers who are so prevalent in the world today. Even a cursory glance at the news reveals the plight of humanity on the move somewhere in the world. At the hands of forces beyond their control people are forced to leave their homes and everything they hold dear for fear of what might happen to them simply by remaining in a place they have always known. Hunted and under constant threat such people seek asylum from those who see life differently. Where, hopefully, they can experience humanity in a different way by receiving safety, security, and refuge.

The good news, to be found in the scriptures, as we celebrate the Holy Family in this Christmas season, is that we continue to discover its true meaning, and it is this which must challenge our lives of faith today. However, if we are truly to achieve this, we must be willing to let go much of that which the secular world wants us to hold dear. For if we are to discover Christ, then he is not to be found in the giving of gifts which we cannot afford, and no-one really wants. Neither is he to be found in gorging ourselves with food, though we are far from being hungry. So, where is the Son of God to be found then? The answer to this is to be discovered right before our eyes in the scriptures, in the word of God itself, if only we would read them. For Jesus is to be found where he has always been, with the refugees and asylum seekers of this world.

*Something to think about or discuss:*

1. *In what ways have we romanticised the story of Christmas?*

2. *Have you ever reflected on what it must have been like for the Holy Family to be on the run?*

3. *Why do you think this account, given to us by Matthew, is used as we celebrate the Holy Family?*

4. *Can you list or name three things we can learn about what it means to be a Christian from this reading?*

5. *In what ways, if any, has this reflection influenced how you think about and react to the plight of refugees and asylum seekers today?*

**Seven:**

**'The God of Second Chances'**

Luke 2:16-21

**Mary, Mother of God**

*So, they went with haste and found Mary and Joseph, and the child lying in the manger. When they saw this, they made known what had been told them about this child; and all who heard it were amazed at what the shepherds told them. But Mary treasured all these words and pondered them in her heart. The shepherds returned, glorifying, and praising God for all they had heard and seen, as it had been told them.*

We have journeyed together through Advent and reflected on the real meaning of Christmas, now we arrive at a New Year. How do we feel? What are your hopes and dreams for this New Year which lies ahead? What about our faith, how do we feel about that? Has our celebration of the birth of Jesus rejuvenated the hope and the trust we place in him? Are we now more conscious than we were before of our call to discipleship and what this might mean? Are we prepared to be challenged, in our calling, as to what it means to bear witness to Christ in the world in which we live? Are we willing to pay the cost of discipleship, and do we understand what this might mean?

One of the things I never grow tired of saying is that to me, at least, God is the God of second chances and therefore with him we can always begin again. Sometimes responding to the call of discipleship can seem so daunting and we can feel so inadequate that we do not even know where to begin. Then there is always that sense of not being good enough. At this point I always call to mind two things, firstly the words of Jesus when he said, *'You have not chosen me, but I chose you.'* (John 15:16) And secondly, the words of Saint Paul in his letter to the Romans, *'Nothing will be able to separate us from the love of God in Christ Jesus Our Lord.'* (Romans 8:39) Both of these quotations from sacred scripture, which is, of course, the word of God speaking directly to each and every single one of us, collectively and individually, serve to remind me that who I am is good enough, and that there is truly nothing I can ever say or do which will separate me from God. Somehow that always makes me feel better. With that in mind let us now turn our attention to the reading for today from Luke.

The first and remarkable thing to note here is how the shepherds having been told by the angel of the glorious birth of the saviour put all their fears to one side as they, *'hurried off and found Mary and Joseph, and the baby, lying in the manger.'* Think for a minute what the angel originally said to the shepherds out on the hillside as the glory of the Lord shone all around. Can you remember? It was, *'do not be afraid.'* The same words which Jesus spoke to his disciples as he appeared to them after the resurrection, the same words the risen Lord spoke to Mary Magdalene in the garden after he had risen from the dead on that first Easter morning, and the same words the angel spoke to Mary at the annunciation. In fact, the words, *'do not be afraid'* occur no less than 365 times in the Bible, it is as if God cannot tell us enough not to let our lives be ruled by fear. As we reflect on a New Year then, perhaps, one of the things we need to keep at the forefront of our minds is not to allow fear to prevent us from bearing witness to Christ. All we have to do, is place all our hope and all our trust, in him.

Secondly, note if you will, the reaction of the shepherds having seen the Christ child lying in the manger with Mary and Joseph nearby, *'When they had seen him, they spread the word concerning what they had been told to them about this child, and all who heard it were amazed at what they the shepherds said to them.'* In other words, those same shepherds who previously had been terrified by the appearance of the angel now became fearless evangelists. What makes this even more remarkable is that in the ancient world shepherds tended to be, largely, uneducated men. Indeed, they spent so much time on the hillside watching over their sheep they often failed to keep the laws of purification, which in the eyes of their own religious leaders, in effect, made them bad Jews. Yet here they were telling everyone what they had seen and heard. We in the same way should not allow fear to prevent us from evangelising but what does this mean for our lives of faith today?

For help let us now turn to Mary and note what our reading tells us about her, '*But Mary treasured all these things and pondered them in her heart.*' Perhaps, this is the first thing that we need to do at the start of a New Year, spend time lovingly with the scriptures, reflecting on what they mean for us in the depths of our own hearts. We often forget that Christ is as present in the scriptures as he is in the sacraments, and it is there we can develop a close and loving relationship with him whilst all the time discerning what he is calling us to be and do. This, in fact, is what I have been encouraging you to do though the pages of this book so far and indeed it is the main reason why I wrote it in the first place. I am convinced that we all need to rediscover a love for God's word and keep it close to our hearts. So, if you do not possess one, I would suggest that you purchase a copy of the Bible and begin a new relationship with it and if I might say so, open a new chapter in your own life, and then see what happens.

Now look at what the shepherds did next, '*The shepherds returned, glorifying and praising God for all the things they had heard and seen, which were just as they had been told.*' In other words, they came back for more, they needed to see the Christ child again, and they needed to go back to the source of all their hope and joy. I would suggest that this is an excellent reason to go back to church. Yes, it can be daunting, and we may well be unfamiliar with what goes on, giving rise to fear but remember the words of the angel to those shepherds, '*Do not be afraid,*' and see what became of them when they overcame their fear. We need to go back to church, however, for two main reasons: firstly, to discover the source of everything - Jesus Christ himself, present in the sacrament, present in his word, and present in his people. And secondly, we need to back to church because we need each other, because we were never meant to be alone, '*for where two or three meet in my name, I am there among them.*' (Matthew 18:20)

You may find this hard and be tempted to say, '*I'm just not good enough!*' But remember where we started this reflection, that God is the God of second chances and that there is nothing we can do or say which will separate us from his love. It is a simple truth that most people, these days, do not read the Bible but they will read us. In the same way most people do not go to church, but they may look to us to see what difference it makes to our lives of faith, and there is the challenge. Perhaps, at the start of this New Year, we can like Mary, *'ponder all of these things in our hearts,'* find the courage to place our hand in the hand of Christ and with him step out of the darkness and into the light.

*Something to think about or discuss:*

1. *What plans, if any, do you have for the New Year?*

2. *How does this reflection make you feel about the practice of your faith and your relationship with God?*

3. *Do you think it is important to have your own copy of the Bible and to spend time reading and pondering its meaning in your heart?*

4. *Can you think of different ways you might put your faith into action this New Year?*

5. *Why do you believe the New Year starts with a celebration devoted to Mary, Mother of God?*

**Eight:**

**'Follow that Star'**

Matthew 2:1-12

**The Epiphany**

*In the time of King Herod, after Jesus was born in Bethlehem of Judea, wise men from the East came to Jerusalem, asking, "Where is the child who has been born king of the Jews? For we observed his star at its rising and have come to pay him homage." When King Herod heard this, he was frightened, and all Jerusalem with him; and calling together all the chief priests and scribes of the people, he inquired of them where the Messiah was to be born. They told him, "In Bethlehem of Judea; for so it has been written by the prophet: 'And you, Bethlehem, in the land of Judah, are by no means least among the rulers of Judah; for from you shall come a ruler who is to shepherd my people, Israel.'"*

*Then Herod secretly called for the wise men and learned from them the exact time when the star had appeared. Then he sent them to Bethlehem, saying, "Go and search diligently for the child; and when you have found him, bring me word so that I may also go and pay him homage." When they had heard the king, they set out; and there, ahead of them, went the star that they had seen at its rising, until it stopped over the place where the child was. When they saw that the star had stopped, they were overwhelmed with joy. On entering the house, they saw the child with Mary his mother; and they knelt down and paid him homage. Then, opening their treasure chests, they offered him gifts of gold, frankincense, and myrrh. And having been warned in a dream not to return to Herod, they left for their own country by another road.'*

Let us start this reflection with some questions and then see what we can do with them:

- Where is the star in our lives?
- Before whom do we kneel and worship?
- What do we place at the feet of the Christ Child?

- Are we alert and responsive to God's invitation to enter into His Kingdom?

- What is the real meaning of the Epiphany?

Now spend some time reflecting on, and answering some, or all of these questions. It might also help to discuss them with others. When you are ready keep your answers in mind as you work your way through the following reflection.

Perhaps, the best place to start is with the Magi themselves and see what we can find out about them which might shed some light on our understanding of the Epiphany. First of all, we know that they came from the East and were pagans, which is to say they were not Jews. Secondly, their homeland was believed to be a place of science and astrology, hence they may well have spent many years studying the night sky in order to make sense out of life on Earth. In other words, these were learned and clever people. Their language, however, was mathematics and science not that of the Hebrew Scriptures. So, guided by an astrological event in the heavens, they set out in search of the truth on a journey that would be long, hard, and demanding in ways, perhaps, they could never have imagined beforehand.

Imagine the scene then when these strange and mysterious figures arrive in Jerusalem. They are, in fact, not just looking for a king but the king of all kings; the universe has revealed him as such. This is something they make clearly known and King Herod is not happy. After all he is the King of the Jews by decree of Rome and there can be no rival to this proclamation. Yet, the Magi have lost their way and need help and who better to provide it than King Herod himself. He, however, is not the one that they seek, and neither is it Caesar Augustus.

The only thing Herod sees is a threat to his privileged status and this is something which he cannot tolerate. The chief priests and scribes tell him that the scriptures point to *'Bethlehem, in the land of Judah,'* as the place where such a child would be born. Now a set of different seekers are sent out to find this new king not with the intention of paying him homage, but rather with ending his life.

This, however, will be an all-too-common feature of Jesus's life. Those in power with status, wealth and privilege will always feel threatened by Jesus because they have the most to lose. Even the religious leaders will resist him because of his common, uneducated, background, refusing to accept the fact, that God could be right there in front of their own eyes. Intolerance and rejection by the powerful and mighty would follow Jesus wherever he went. Only those who had been stripped of every human dignity were open to his proclamation of the Kingdom of Heaven with its powerful message of mercy, forgiveness, compassion, and love.

Eventually the Magi regain their direction, follow the star, and reach their destination. Their long journey has involved ups and downs, at times they have lost their way, seeking help and guidance elsewhere. Yet we are told plainly, that when they did see the star, *'they were overjoyed.'* Perhaps, this is something we can learn from too. On discovering the child their first reaction was to, *'bow down and worship him.'* At this point, I cannot help but ask, was this what they were expecting? A stable, animals, shepherds, and a manger along with two simple parents, Mary, and Joseph. Yet the text is quite clear, they have found the one whom they have been searching for their whole lives. What happens next is, of course, quite remarkable because they place before the child everything in life, they value most. In doing so, these Magi from the East, these scientists and mathematicians, these pagans recognise the child before them as not only their King but also their Lord.

What a story this is and, perhaps, one that we are very familiar with but now let us reflect a little more on what it might mean for our lives of faith today. Remember those questions we asked right at the beginning of this reflection, let us now return to them having explored in some detail what happened at the Epiphany. I will not, however, provide any answers to the questions I am about to invite you to ponder. Instead, all I ask is that you spend some time with the text and this reflection before proceeding to answer some or all of the following questions.

*Something to think about or discuss:*

1. *What leads us to Christ now or where is the star in our own lives today?*

2. *Where is God in our list of priorities or before whom do we kneel and worship?*

3. *What do we value the most in life and therefore place at the feet of the Christ Child?*

4. *How open are we to Our Lord's invitation to enter His Kingdom and what does this mean?*

5. *Can we explain what the real meaning of the Epiphany is for the world today*

# Nine:

## 'Led by the Spirit'

Matthew 3:13-17

## The Baptism of the Lord

*Then Jesus came from Galilee to John at the Jordan, to be baptized by him. John would have prevented him, saying, "I need to be baptized by you, and do you come to me?" But Jesus answered him, "Let it be so now; for it is proper for us in this way to fulfil all righteousness." Then he consented. And when Jesus had been baptized, just as he came up from the water, suddenly the heavens were opened to him, and he saw the Spirit of God descending like a dove and alighting on him. And a voice from heaven said, "This is my Son, the Beloved, with whom I am well pleased."*

There can be little doubt that the baptism of Jesus caused some controversy in the early days of Christianity, after all, *'why did the sinless Son of God need to be baptised?'* It is a question I still get asked, quite often, even today. However, one way of approaching the issue is to see things in reverse or to ask a question of our own, *'why would Matthew include the baptism of Jesus in his Gospel if it was not true?'* There must, therefore, be a reason for finding this important event at the very start of Jesus's ministry and now we need to find out why?

Perhaps, the first point to make is that Matthew needs to make something abundantly clear right from the start of Jesus's ministry, that he is not a disciple of John. So, look at what John the Baptist says upon seeing Jesus for the first time, *'I need to be baptised by you, and do you come to me?'* Here we see a clear recognition as to the superiority of Jesus over John. Yet, Jesus goes on to say, *'Let it be so now, for it is proper for us to do this to fulfil all righteousness.'* However, the most significant part of the proceedings happens once Jesus emerges from the water when we are told, *'At that moment heaven was opened, and he saw the Spirit of God descending like a dove and lighting on him.'* The key words for us here are, the *'Spirit of God'* which comes down only on Jesus. For only he can be baptised with the Holy Spirit and, of course, what happens next changes everything because the voice from heaven identifies Jesus with the words, *'This is my Son.'*

Quite clearly then Jesus is not a prophet like John, nor is he just another one of his disciples and neither is he like everyone else who joined the queue that day, on the banks of the river Jordan, waiting to be baptised. Rather he is nothing less than the Son of God himself, the beloved one, in whom the Father is, *'well pleased.'* Matthew wants to remove, right from the start, any confusion as to who Jesus might be by, in one sense, starting with that which he is not. Therefore, he is not a prophet, he is not a disciple, and he is not a scribe or Pharisee or Sadducee or any other kind of leader which belongs to the religious establishment of the day. No, he is none of these because he is the only Son of the Father, whom the Father loves and is well pleased with.

Now we need to return to the importance of the *'Spirit of God'* which comes down only on Jesus. This takes us right back to the beginning of everything, creation itself, and therefore the book of Genesis. Here Matthew is describing the breath of God which is the source of everything because it both creates and sustains all life. It is through this same *'Spirit'* that God continues to express both his love for creation whilst at the same time renewing and transforming it. This now means that it is through Jesus that God will be revealed to the world and his life, death, and resurrection will make all things new.

Full of the life-giving *'Spirit'* of his Father Jesus will confront evil and defeat it, whilst at the same time healing the sick, raising the dead, and by welcoming those who are despised, rejected and unloved, even by their own religious leaders, into the Kingdom of Heaven. He will exclude no one and include everyone. As a result, there will be no condemnation in him because he comes only to bless and reassure that God is closer to the people than they could ever imagine and loves them more than they could ever know. In essence, filled with the *'Spirit'* Jesus comes to set humanity free from sin, offering in its place the life only God can give.

It is because of this that Jesus made a deep impression on the lives of those early Christians as they saw in him a life lived differently, full of the '*Spirit.*' He would teach them with authority, yet his way would be the way of mercy, compassion, forgiveness, and love. Above all, Jesus would open the way back to the Father for all people by simply inviting everyone to place all their hope and all their trust in him.

What does this mean for our lives of faith today then? Well, the remarkable truth is that the same '*Spirt*' which descended on Jesus at his baptism is also available to us as his disciples in the world today. It is therefore to this same '*Spirit*' that we must now turn to and rely on just as Jesus did. In the same way this '*Spirit*' must be the inspiration behind everything we do whether that be as individual Christians, or the church and equally it must be clearly visible for all to see. How will the '*Spirit*' be recognised in our lives today? Well, the answer to that is quite simple. This is because when people see us our lives bear witness to Jesus, we will be engaged today in exactly what he did two millennia ago. Thus, we will be serving the poor and the needy, speaking out on behalf of the voiceless and the oppressed, campaigning for those whose human rights have been violated, visiting those who are sick or in prison, welcoming the stranger and rejecting all forms of evil. In this way Jesus continues to live in and through his disciples today because his '*Spirit*' is constantly being poured out into our hearts and this must be reflected now in our lives of faith.

*Something to think about or discuss:*

1. *Explain why Jesus had to be baptised.*

2. *Do you think it is important for people to be baptised today and explain why?*

3. *What made Jesus unique?*

4. *What signs are there that 'Spirt of God' is alive and active in the world today?*

5. *Are we dependant on the 'Spirit of God' in our lives of faith today? What can be done to rediscover our need for God?*

# Year B:

# Mark

*'Therefore, keep awake for you do not know when the master of the house will come, in the evening, or at midnight, or at cockcrow, or at dawn, or else he may find you asleep when he comes suddenly. And what I say to you I say to all: Keep awake.'*
*(Mark 13:35-37)*

# Mark and Advent

As we enter Year B of the liturgical cycle we are hit with a real sense of urgency. First of all, Mark tells us to, *'Watch!'* Continuing with the same theme we are then told to, *'Be on your guard! Be alert. You do not know when that time will come.'* In this way we are being prepared to enter the season of Advent with a challenge as we wait, in anticipation, for the coming of the Lord. The nature of such a demand confronts each and every single one of us to ask, if the Lord were to return, can I hand on heart, say that I am truly ready?

So, what are we to do in preparation for the celebration of Jesus's birth at Christmas? Once again, it is John the Baptist who tells us to be converted by having a complete change of heart. But what does this mean for us today? When was the last time we plummeted the depths of our own hearts? When was the last time we reflected, deeply, on our complete need for God? When was the last time we identified those things in our lives which prevented us from having a personal relationship with Christ? Perhaps then, this is the season in which we need to be brave and honest with ourselves by recognising and admitting our own blindness. For this reason, the starting point might well be with the sacrament of reconciliation.

As we move through Advent the Gospels encourage us to deepen our relationship with God but the biggest hindrance to this can often be our unwillingness to let God be God. At first, this might be quite a strange thing to say, but give it time and see what happens. After all, how many of us want to turn God into something we want him to be rather than embracing him for who he is. Advent invites us to return to God through his Son by recognising that he is the one who comes in search of us, simply because he loves us. All we need to do is let go and allow his love to penetrate our hearts.

Finally, we come to the end of Advent with our eyes open and our hearts ready to discover something completely different. For God is closer to us than we could ever imagine and loves us more than we could ever know. But where do we look for him? The answer to this question is to be found in the least likely of places. After all who would have ever thought that the Son of God could be born in a stable and placed in a manger?

# One:

## 'Keep Watch'

Mark 13:33-37

### First Sunday of Advent

*Beware, keep alert; for you do not know when the time will come. It is like a man going on a journey, when he leaves home and puts his slaves in charge, each with his work, and commands the doorkeeper to be on the watch. Therefore, keep awake for you do not know when the master of the house will come, in the evening, or at midnight, or at cockcrow, or at dawn, or else he may find you asleep when he comes suddenly. And what I say to you I say to all: Keep awake.*

It might seem an odd question to ask myself but am I asleep? Putting it a slightly different way, have I become comfortable with my faith in Jesus Christ? In today's Gospel reading we are literally told to, *'Watch!'* So, as we start the season of Advent, I am going to spend some time, in this reflection, trying to understand what this exactly means.

It is now well over two thousand years since Jesus walked the earth and a lot has happened since then, but his words are not only the words of life they are, in fact, timeless too. It is for this reason, therefore, that they are as relevant today as they ever were. But there is a problem and perhaps it starts with me. After all, how do I really feel about my faith? Does my heart burn within me as I read his words now? If not, why not and what can I do about it? So, I decided to go right back to the beginning and made a remarkable discovery. Take a moment or two, to read, again, the Gospel reading for today. What you find is an urgency not only in what is being said but in its very tone, *'Be on your guard! Be alert. You do not know when that time will come.'* See what I mean?

This led to the early Christians focusing much of their time, energy, and effort on the belief that Jesus would return any minute. Perhaps, this was a reflection of their great hope and need to be with him as soon as possible. Yet as time went by there developed a creeping realisation that for some reason, unknown to them, the Lord's coming was delayed. The longer this went on, the more of a problem it presented, in so far as, their enthusiasm was beginning to wane. What would happen if they began to forget Jesus? The very source of the fire, which fuelled their faith, was in danger of going out. They were, in fact, falling asleep and were concerned that this is how Jesus would find them when he returned. So, what were they to do? In a strange kind of way discovering this truth brought me a sense of comfort and consolation because if those early Christians felt like this, then perhaps my own feelings were not so bad after all. However, the question remained, what to do about it?

When we go back to the Gospel reading, we find the answer staring at us, right in the face, because the refrain is repeated constantly, *'Watch, and remain alert and stay awake.'* Yet, there is something else, which is quite easy to miss but which speaks directly to us all, across time, making it as relevant today as it was then, over two thousand years ago, and it is this, *'What I say to you, I say to everyone: Watch!'* There we have it, Jesus speaking directly to all of us, but is it, in fact, a warning?

Now we can come back to the present and begin to unpack what all of this means for those of us who follow Jesus today. So, first and foremost we must all ask ourselves, are we awake, on watch and alert? Is our faith alive or is it in fact, and in all honesty, slowly dying just like those early Christians feared theirs was all those centuries ago? If any of this is true, what can we do about it on this first Sunday in Advent? After all, it is today that we begin our preparations for that holiest of seasons, Christmas. Perhaps, we need to begin by being totally honest with ourselves and admit that we simply cannot go on like this, being too comfortable in our faith. We need to *'wake up, be on the alert,'* and start to challenge ourselves by shaking off the comfortable nature of what we believe in and replace it with something which is alive.

There is one very simple answer to all of these questions, and it is, Jesus. On this first Sunday of Advent let us be alert to his presence in our lives and watchful for his face amongst us today.

We need to cling to him and the best way to do this is to fall in love with him again so that his heart merges with ours. In this way our lives will be transformed by his grace setting our hearts on fire with the flame of his most perfect love. Think, for a second, how important light is during Advent. Reflect on how light drives back the darkness and believe that Christ is, in fact, not just the light but the source of the light. We must, above and beyond all things, deepen our relationship with Jesus so that in the words of Saint Paul, *'It is no longer I who live but Christ who lives in me.'* (Galatians 2:20) Think of it like this, what will attract others to Christ? A church which is asleep or one which is on fire with the love of Christ? Those early Christians, all those centuries ago, realised that they were in danger of losing their relationship with Jesus as they slowly fell asleep. It was, however, the Word of God, which pulled them back and infused them with enthusiasm for Christ. It is this which we must rediscover anew today. The message is the same, it will not change, *'Watch, and remain alert and stay awake.'* Only Jesus can lead us back to the Father. Only Jesus can fill our hearts with such joy that at the very mention of his name we fall to our knees. Only Jesus can give such meaning, purpose, and value to our lives that without him we simply cannot live. Filled with such creative joy, and during this Advent season, it is time now to reflect what we believe in how we live. And if we can do that, be sure of one thing, others will come.

*Something to think about or discuss:*

1. *How are we asleep in the practice of our faith today?*

2. *Would you describe the church as being asleep? If yes, how?*

3. *In what ways can we, 'Watch, and remain alert and stay awake?'*

4. *How can we stir up our faith in Christ this Advent so that it impacts on our lives?*

5. *What must we do, as a church, and as individuals to bring others to Christ?*

**Two:**

**'Conversion – Me?'**

Mark 1:1-8

**Second Sunday of Advent**

*The beginning of the good news of Jesus Christ, the Son of God. As it is written in the prophet Isaiah, "See, I am sending my messenger ahead of you, who will prepare your way; the voice of one crying out in the wilderness: 'Prepare the way of the Lord, make his paths straight,'"*

*John the baptizer appeared in the wilderness, proclaiming a baptism of repentance for the forgiveness of sins. And people from the whole Judean countryside and all the people of Jerusalem were going out to him, and were baptized by him in the river Jordan, confessing their sins. Now John was clothed with camel's hair, with a leather belt around his waist, and he ate locusts and wild honey. He proclaimed, "The one who is more powerful than I is coming after me; I am not worthy to stoop down and untie the thong of his sandals. I have baptized you with water; but he will baptize you with the Holy Spirit."*

When you hear the word conversion what does it make you think of? I cannot speak for others, but I have a tendency to always apply it to someone else. After all, I see myself as a Christian, so what has conversion got, personally, to do with me? However, has thinking like this caused me to miss the point of what true conversion is really about? And am I reducing conversion to one specific moment in my life, if so when was it? You see I was baptised when I was about six weeks old and was brought up as a Christian, so when did my conversion happen? Do you see what I mean? Now I am asking all of these questions against the background of today's Gospel reading, which features prominently the ministry of John the Baptist. This year, I am going to take a look at things with fresh eyes and see what happens.

The Gospel opens with some remarkable words, *'The beginning of the good news about Jesus Christ, the Son of God.'* In these words, Mark summarises what his Gospel is all about, that Jesus is the Son of God. In reading them, however, what effect do they have on me and my life of faith today? After all, I have read them so many times before, but have they lost their impact? Do I take them for granted? Is there something I should be doing now to understand and appreciate the dramatic essence of what Mark is actually proclaiming? Perhaps, there is no better time to ask such questions than on this Second Sunday of Advent.

As always though I find myself going back to the actual text. Just after Mark delivers his dramatic good news there is a complete change of tone and what follows is nothing less than a warning and it is urgent, so we had better take note and listen. If the people are to receive the Messiah, then they must be converted. Equally, if I am to really understand the meaning of Mark's opening sentence about Jesus being the Son of God then, perhaps, I need to be converted too.

On the scene now arrives John the Baptist and his mission is to prepare the way for the coming of the Lord. Could it be that I need to listen, afresh, to the words of this great prophet in a new way and undergo my own conversion of heart if I am truly to prepare myself for the coming of the Lord at Christmas? John's message is hugely powerful in so far as he is not just preparing individuals for the coming of the Messiah but the whole of humanity, for all time. This is why his message, and his method of delivery is so radically different. Gone are the old ways, this way is new. Do not look for the expected but rather for the unexpected. Be prepared to look beyond the conventional for something which tears down all that which is familiar. This is the power of John's message, but he is not the one, rather he has come to prepare the way for the one who, when he comes, will change everything.

The next thing to do is to look at and reflect upon how the people react to John's prophetic message. Mark tells us that the people come from Judea and Jerusalem finding their way into the desert attracted by John's uncompromising and powerful message. The desert was, of course, the place where their ancestors were bound to each other and God in the deepest of all relationships; the covenant. John's invitation is to change or to be prepared to undergo a complete transformation of heart. In other words, John calls upon the people to be converted. But what does this mean both then and now? The call to conversion is, perhaps, at least at first, an invitation to recognise that things need to change. This means me appreciating that there are things within me, what I say, do and even think, which prevent me from being who God calls me to be. This is sin, something which I need to acknowledge, personally, without judging or condemning others and with which comes a cry from the heart recognising I need to be saved. For this reason, the people came to John on the banks of the river Jordan, confessed their sins and were baptised.

Now we need to apply this to our own lives of faith today but where do we start? Perhaps, the best place to begin is with own souls, that part of us which belongs to God and defines who we are. In many ways this is the actual problem because how many of us gives any attention to our souls? Think about it for a second and apply it to your own life and you will see what I mean. The question I am trying to ask here is how many of us really place Christ at the very heart of our lives? I would also apply this to the life of the church. It is now that we arrive at the very core of John the Baptist's message, which challenges us to search the very depths of our soul to discover the truth about our faith and it all comes down to this, does Christ give meaning, purpose and value to my life and can I live without him? To answer a question such as this calls for total honesty and most of us are not brave enough, not strong enough even, to do that. It is this, I am suggesting, what John the Baptist is inviting us to do. Our response must involve a great deal of soul searching, perhaps over a long period of time, leading eventually to inner change or transformation. This, however, is what is meant by conversion because it leads to transformed existence. Now our lives conform to that of Christ so that others see him in us, which again echoes the words of Saint Paul, *'Yet it is no longer I who live, but Christ who lives in me.'* (Galatians 2:20) In this way, Jesus is placed at both the centre of lives and that of the Church.

However, let us now be honest with ourselves, most of us will not go into the desert or engage in such soul searching. Most of us will avoid conversion and ignore any voice calling us to change. This is because most of us are afraid and lack the courage to recognise the enormity, and the implications, of Mark's opening sentence and John's call for conversion. Just for a moment go back to that figure of John standing on the banks of the river Jordan with thousands of people flocking to him, all of whom recognised their own need to be converted, the starting point for which was the confession of their own sins. It is a truly remarkable and inspiring sight.

Right, now let us come back to ourselves on this second Sunday of Advent and ask, what should we do, and where should we start? My answer is a very simple and straight-forward one, but you might not like it. Seek the sacrament of reconciliation or confession, and in so doing seek God's mercy and forgiveness and if you cannot do that, well there lies the problem and that is, perhaps, why things just do not change. But it does not have to be that way, does it?

*Something to think about or discuss:*

1. *What does the word 'conversion' mean to you?*

2. *Why do you think John the Baptist called the people to be 'converted?'*

3. *Is Christ really at the centre of our lives, and that of the church? If so, how?*

4. *Why do you think many people have stopped coming to church?*

5. *How important is the sacrament of reconciliation in the life of Christians today?*

**Three:**

## 'Let God be God'

John 1:6-8, 19-28

**Third Sunday of Advent**

*There was a man sent from God, whose name was John. He came as a witness to testify to the light, so that all might believe through him. He himself was not the light, but he came to testify to the light.*

*This is the testimony given by John when the Jews sent priests and Levites from Jerusalem to ask him, "Who are you?" He confessed and did not deny it, but confessed, "I am not the Messiah." And they asked him, "What then? Are you Elijah?" He said, "I am not." "Are you the prophet?" He answered, "No." Then they said to him, "Who are you? Let us have an answer for those who sent us. What do you say about yourself?" He said, "I am the voice of one crying out in the wilderness, 'Make straight the way of the Lord,'" as the prophet Isaiah said.*

*Now they had been sent from the Pharisees. They asked him, "Why then are you baptizing if you are neither the Messiah, nor Elijah, nor the prophet?" John answered them, "I baptize with water. Among you stands one whom you do not know, the one who is coming after me; I am not worthy to untie the thong of his sandal." This took place in Bethany across the Jordan where John was baptizing.*

As we enter the third week of Advent and, *yes,* Christmas is that close, we need to get something perfectly clear. We are not the light, and we are not the source of the light either. This was something John the Baptist understood right from the beginning when we are told, *'He came as a witness to testify concerning the light.'* As if to emphasise this, even further, we are also told later, *'He himself was not the light; he came only as a witness to the light.'* You see John wanted the people to understand something crucial, that Jesus was, in fact, amongst them now. As we said in our previous reflection, crowds of people came to John seeking baptism. However, he made it very clear, as we can see in our Gospel reading for today, that he was not, in fact, the one they were really looking for. Instead, Jesus was amongst them, waiting for that moment when his true presence would be fully revealed. In this respect John's role was very clear, to prepare the way for the coming of Jesus so that the people might see and believe in him.

All this seems straight forward, and you might be thinking that there does not appear to be anything new here but wait a minute and take another look at the text. John makes the point to the people that Jesus is, in fact, amongst them and yet remains unknown. Now here is the serious question I want us to think about and reflect upon this Third Sunday of Advent - is Jesus with us here and now in our very midst, and do we really recognise him? Indeed, what type of Jesus do we really believe in, follow, and commit our lives to? Think about it for yourself and see what kind of answers you come up with. I remember Gerard Hughes once saying that the problem with the Church, Christians and Jesus is that we have domesticated him. We have taken him, placed him in a cupboard, locked the door and turned Jesus into something we want him to be. This is a crucial point because how often, in our lives and in the life of the church, is Jesus relegated to the background? There he can rest in safety, until, when it suits us, we can bring him out, but if his teaching does not quite fit our point of view or our need, we can put him back in the cupboard where he can cause no harm. When this happens, often without realising it, we replace his light with our own. Now, how often do we do that – I wonder?

This is an extremely challenging thing to say but the early Christians were very clear about who John the Baptist was and his role in preparing the way for the coming of Jesus, whereby one thing is absolutely certain, he was not the light. Only Jesus is the light and not just the light but the very source of it. So, what does this mean for those who would follow Christ today? I would say that one thing is certain, and it is this – we must go back to Christ and let his light shine. Our lives of faith must conform to his so that his light shines through us. Go back, if you will, to the point we made earlier about John's teaching that Jesus was in the midst of the people even as they stood on the banks of the river Jordan.

In the same way Jesus is in our midst today but most people cannot or will not recognise him and much of that is our own fault. Why, might you ask? Because we have turned him into something we want him to be rather than letting *'God be God.'*

Yet the solution is a very simple one and it lies in our own hands. All we have to do is become more like Jesus. John pointed to Christ not himself. John prepared the way for the coming of Jesus not himself. John said Jesus was the light not he. John witnessed to the light so that through Jesus and Jesus alone, *'All might believe.'* It is this kind of attitude that we need to recapture if we are to be authentic witnesses to Christ. Firstly, however, we need to recognise that Jesus is in our midst and make every effort to truly know him. Secondly, we need to make sure that it is Jesus we witness to rather than ourselves.

You might say and, to be honest, I would not blame you that we have heard all of this before, but have you? What I am really talking about here is conforming our hearts to the heart of Jesus. That for me, at least, is what being a Christian, which is to say a follower of Christ, really means. Yet have we not in the words of Gerard Hughes, put Jesus in the cupboard where we can keep him at a safe distance, control him and from where he is no threat. Such a Jesus has no real impact on our lives and following him costs us nothing because we are doing it on our own terms. Try this as a test and see what happens. Does Jesus give meaning, purpose, and value to your life? What demands, if any, does following Christ place on you? When was the last time you put your faith first and it cost you? When others look at you, can you honestly say that they see reflected in your life and the way in which you live, the light of Christ? Does your relationship with Jesus enliven you, enthuse you and fill you with a desire to love and serve others in his name? In what ways has your following of Christ left a deep impression on you as a person? Now can you still say, I have heard all of this before?

The good news is that with God we can always begin again, and it is never too late to start over. So, here we are on the Third Sunday of Advent, and we need to make a simple, life changing, decision. Can we return to Jesus anew, and discover something that was always there but we were too afraid to admit? Ultimately, the good news Mark opens his Gospel with is that with the coming of Jesus everything changes and that here, right before our very eyes, is God. In so doing Jesus reveals not only the nature and being of God but also what it means to be a human being fully alive. This is what both the church and the world need now perhaps more than ever. What I am going to say now, therefore, because of this, might shock some people, but it proclaims the good news and therefore must be said. We, as the follows of Christ today, must conform our lives to his to the point that we speak like him, act like him, serve like him and love like him. His compassion must be our compassion, his forgiveness our forgiveness and his mercy our mercy too. Equally, just like Jesus, we must also place all our trust in the Father praying that, *'His will be done.'*

Living faith-filled lives like this will fill our hearts with joy as his light shines through us lighting up the darkness of the world. Then an amazing truth is revealed which takes us right back to John the Baptist on the banks of the river Jordan all those centuries ago. That Christ is, in fact, in our midst here and now living, loving, and serving others through us. Yet, why do we find this so hard to believe, let alone live? Thomas Merton once said, it is because of fear that we fail to follow Jesus, and therefore let God be God. Our nature is crippled because we are afraid to love, and we do not dare to be human. It is against this temptation most of all that the disciple of Jesus must labour with inexhaustible love.

To finish this reflection I would ask you, in this season of Advent, to spend some time sitting still in front of a burning candle. Hear again the words of the Gospel telling us about the mission of John the Baptist, *'He came as a witness to testify concerning the light,'* and *'He himself was not the light; he came only as a witness to the light.'* Note how the candle will burn itself out to provide light and so push back the darkness, just as Jesus gave his life completely so that we might share in it. We might not be the light, but we can reflect something of his light, and we might not be the word, but we can be a voice, along with that of John the Baptist, which simply invites others to know that Christ is, in fact, in our midst.

*Something to think about or discuss:*

    *1. How is Jesus in our midst today? Can you think of specific examples?*

    *2. In what ways do we seek to control God? Why would we do this?*

    *3. Why are we afraid to be like Jesus? Does this prevent us from being truly human?*

    *4. How would you describe your relationship with Jesus? Why is this important?*

    *5. Is Jesus at the centre of the Church in everything it does? Should he be? If so, why?*

**Four:**

## 'Are You Ready for Something Completely Different?'

Luke 1:26-38

## Fourth Sunday of Advent

*In the sixth month the angel Gabriel was sent by God to a town in Galilee called Nazareth, to a virgin engaged to a man whose name was Joseph, of the house of David. The virgin's name was Mary. And he came to her and said, "Greetings, favoured one! The Lord is with you." But she was much perplexed by his words and pondered what sort of greeting this might be. The angel said to her, "Do not be afraid, Mary, for you have found favour with God. And now, you will conceive in your womb and bear a son, and you will name him Jesus. He will be great and will be called the Son of the Most High, and the Lord God will give to him the throne of his ancestor David. He will reign over the house of Jacob forever, and of his kingdom there will be no end." Mary said to the angel, "How can this be since I am a virgin? The angel said to her, "The Holy Spirit will come upon you, and the power of the Most High will overshadow you; therefore, the child to be born will be holy; he will be called Son of God. And now, your relative Elizabeth in her old age has also conceived a son; and this is the sixth month for her who was said to be barren. For nothing will be impossible with God." Then Mary said, "Here am I, the servant of the Lord; let it be with me according to your word." Then the angel departed from her.*

Our last two reflections have concentrated our attention on the figure of John the Baptist preparing the way for the coming of Jesus. On this Fourth Sunday of Advent Luke introduces us to the birth of Jesus for the first time. I can almost hear the Gospel writer say, *'and now for something completely different.'* Yet, even now, we cannot forget the person of John the Baptist and I do not think that the Gospel writers want us too either. For this reason, we can discover something completely new and remarkable when we contrast the birth of John with that of Jesus. Indeed, I would go as far as to say that this is exactly what the Gospel writers are inviting us to do, so that we may truly anticipate what the birth of Jesus means. Nowhere is this more appropriate than on the

Fourth Sunday of Advent.

First and foremost, the announcement of John's birth takes place in the holy city of Jerusalem, the capital of God's people. The birth of Jesus, however, is announced in an obscure, almost unknown village, in the Galilean hillside. This small, insignificant place, far from Jerusalem has no magnificence attached to it. In fact, no one expects anything good to come out of such a place or such a region. Yet it is here that Jesus will live and grow up, read from the scroll of the prophet Isaiah, and associate himself and his ministry with that of the Messiah. On the other hand, Jerusalem will reject him. What might God be telling us here? Perhaps, that we should look for him in the very places the world would least expect to find him. In the obscure, the insignificant, the nothings and the nobodies. Something to think about and reflect upon as we prepare to celebrate our saviour's birth.

When John's birth is announced, it takes place within the walls of the temple, the most sacred and therefore holiest place on earth for the Jews. Indeed, it was the place where God dwelt with his people. The birth of Jesus, however, is announced in a simple dwelling the details of which we know nothing about. In the same way, Jesus will choose to live his life in and with the ordinary working people of his day. In fact, he will share their lives, offering them the mercy, forgiveness, compassion, and love of God. Could it be that the Gospel writers here are asking us to come to a remarkable conclusion? That God is not to be found in magnificent buildings, as important as they might be, but amongst us, here and now. Remember, for a moment, what we said about John the Baptist in a previous reflection? That he, from the banks of the river Jordan, was telling the people that God was in their midst but to recognise him conversion was needed. God shares our lives, in flesh and blood, here and now but we need the eyes of faith to recognise him. Search for God then in the ordinary events of your everyday life and see what happens. After all who would have thought that the Son of God could be born in a stable and placed in a manager? Yet, if we look close enough at the scriptures, it should come, in fact, as no surprise at all.

When we turn to the announcement of John's birth, once again, compared to that of Jesus we are given a remarkable insight into the nature and being of God. This is because the announcement of John's birth is received by a male priest, Zechariah. In fact, it takes place during a solemn ritual which is being celebrated in the temple. On the other hand, when we turn to the announcement of Jesus's birth, it is to a young, unknown, and unimportant girl, Mary by name. We are not told what she is doing, and she obviously has very little, if any, status. This is because the world and culture into which Jesus is to be born has little interest in women. They, in fact, occupy the lowest positions in society and when it comes to matters of faith are often viewed with contempt. Yet, Jesus, as the Son of God, will reverse this attitude treating women with the dignity and respect they deserve. In fact, Mary, is often found constantly with Jesus's disciples and she will be there at the foot of the cross, as he dies, as well as in the upper room, when the Holy Spirit is poured out at Pentecost.

On this Fourth Sunday of Advent then, the readings are preparing us for the celebration of Jesus's birth, which is, in truth, something completely different. In this final reflection before Christmas, we are beginning to understand what this is but there is still one more thing to explore. John, we are told, will be the son of an infertile couple, Zechariah and Elizabeth, something which had happened before, though still blessed by God. Jesus, however, will be conceived through the Holy Spirit, whilst his young mother, Mary, would remain a virgin, something which had never happened before. For this reason, he will be the Son of God and the Saviour of the world. In his birth we are seeing a communion the like of which had never happened before, of that between God and humanity. Think of it like this, the birth of John the Baptist, though aided by God was still as a result of a union between a woman and a man. The birth of Jesus, however, came as a result of God's direct intervention in human history through which he offers the world the gift of his Son. This is what makes the birth of Jesus completely different, and it is for this which we must now prepare our hearts and minds. John issued a call for conversion, and this is why. Let this Christmas not just be another one which passes us by, but rather let it be the moment when we realise, perhaps, for the first time, that the birth of Jesus changes everything including you and me.

*Something to think about or discuss:*

1. *Why do you think the title for this reflection is called,*
   *'Are you ready for something completely different?'*

2. *What do you think is the main message of the Gospel reading*
   *for the Fourth Sunday of Advent?*

3. *Is it useful to compare the birth of John the Baptist with that of Jesus?*
   *If so, why?*

4. *Explain how the birth of Jesus is a gift to humanity.*
   *Why might this be important?*

5. *Has this reflection prepared you for the celebration of Christmas?*
   *Can you explain how and why?*

# Mark and Christmas

As always, it is important to make the point, that although we are now in Year B with the Gospel readings coming primarily from Mark throughout the year, during the Christmas season Matthew, Luke and John all lend a helping hand in telling the story of the incarnation and its significance for our lives of faith today.

We begin, therefore, with the Gospel of John and the great prologue in which he tells us of the pre-existence of Christ and of the significance of why the Son of God became flesh. Here we learn the dramatic truth of what God actually looks like, and what this means for our lives of faith today. The dramatic good news here is that God shares our life so that we might share in his, not just for now, but for the whole of eternity.

However, recognising the Christ in our midst is not easy and this is why Luke wants us to reflect on the need to search for him in the least likely of places and people. For many of us this will involve struggle and a complete change of heart, but God waits for us to find him because he, in fact, is the one who came in search of us first. For the God of Jesus Christ is always present and never absent but the question remains, do we have the eyes of faith to see him? Perhaps, one way to do this is to turn to Mary, Mother of Jesus, asking for her help, support, and guidance. This is because any devotion to Mary will always lead us to her son. Equally, Mary also serves to remind us of the churches need for the feminine without which our lives of faith can never be complete. In this way mother and child point to the deep truth of our relationship with God in and through his Son, which ultimately, is one of intimacy, but above all love.

The Epiphany serves to remind us of our need to let go of everything by placing all our hope and trust in God. We are all on a journey of faith guided by the star, but so very often we lose our way in the maze of life by holding on to those things which prevent us from recognising the God who never leaves our side. What then do we really worship and how can we find our way back? Here the Magi show us the way. This is where the key to everything is, perhaps, the Holy Spirit, which we reflect on through the Baptism of the Lord. Now more than ever we need to rediscover the life given to us at our own baptism, one which enables us to do nothing less than share in the life of God himself. If only we could live the life that God invites us to, in him, because on that day everything would change forever.

It is time now to begin our journey into the season of Christmas, and what lies ahead might just lead to our own transformed existence and the fullness of life, which, of course, only God can give.

# Five:

## 'This is What God Looks Like'

John 1:1-18

### Christmas Day

*In the beginning was the Word, and the Word was with God, and the Word was God. He was in the beginning with God. All things came into being through him, and without him not one thing came into being. What has come into being in him was life, and the life was the light of all people. The light shines in the darkness, and the darkness did not overcome it.*

*There was a man sent from God, whose name was John. He came as a witness to testify to the light, so that all might believe through him. He himself was not the light, but he came to testify to the light. The true light, which enlightens everyone, was coming into the world.*

*He was in the world, and the world came into being through him; yet the world did not know him. He came to what was his own, and his own people did not accept him. But to all who received him, who believed in his name, he gave power to become children of God, who were born, not of blood or of the will of the flesh or of the will of man, but of God.*

*And the Word became flesh and lived among us, and we have seen his glory, the glory as of a father's only son, full of grace and truth. (John testified to him and cried out, "This was he of whom I said, 'He who comes after me ranks ahead of me because he was before me.'") From his fullness we have all received, grace upon grace. The law indeed was given through Moses; grace and truth came through Jesus Christ. No one has ever seen God. It is God the only Son, who is close to the Father's heart, who has made him known.*

One of the first things we need to realise as we celebrate the birth of Jesus at Christmas is that God comes in search of us. God comes to look for us. God comes to seek us out. And why would God do this? Simply because he loves us more than we could ever possibly know. The reading for Christmas day which comes from the prologue to John's Gospel deepens our understanding of who God is through the sending of his Son. Let us now, together, reflect on some of the words of this most profound expression of our faith.

We are told right from the beginning that, *'The Word of God was made flesh.'* In other words, God is not silent but has a deep desire for us to know him. Hence, he speaks directly to us through his Son as an expression of his love for us. Such love is intimate because it takes human form in the flesh and blood of Jesus Christ. It is, therefore, in this way that the divine seeks to share his very life with ours and in so doing reveals that which has remained a mystery up until now, his plan for the salvation of the world. In this way each and every single one of us will be touched by the mercy, compassion, forgiveness, and love of God. This is possible because in Christ, God himself, has become one of us, and one with us, in flesh and blood. The early church fathers expressed it like this, *'God has shared our life so that we might share his.'* This, in fact, is the goal of all human life and explains fully the incarnation and what it means for humanity. What a way to start our celebration of Christmas, to know and believe that God lives in and through us.

What we find here also is the simplicity of God, in so far as, he reduces everything to a person, Jesus. Some of us spend a lot of our time making the faith unnecessarily complicated but ultimately it all comes down to the love of God expressed to us through his Son. As a result, and I cannot say this enough, especially at Christmas, our faith is meant to be simple. So, at this point just stop and pause reflecting on how the love of God was made visible in the flesh and blood of his Son. Yes, God took our flesh and our blood unto himself becoming in the process one of us so that he could, literally, reach out and touch us with that self-same love.

Many of us are tempted to see God as a distant figure who has very little to do with our lives here on earth. Yet the truth is, that through the sending of his Son, God has bridged this gap for all time. Hence, to encounter God directly, all we have to do, is to go to Jesus. Once again, it is as simple as that. Later in the Gospel of John Jesus will say, *'I and the Father are one. To have seen me is to have seen the Father, to have heard me is to have heard the Father.'* Equally, John also tells us that Jesus is, *'the way, the truth and the life.'* Yet, it is at the beginning of the Gospel that this marvellous truth is revealed when we read, *'The word became flesh and dwelt among us.'* It is incredible to say that on this Christmas day God does something the like of which he has never done before, throughout the whole of scripture, and that is reveal himself fully. Therefore, we can claim something quite remarkable about our faith on this most special of days, which is that through the birth of Jesus Christ, God is made fully known. Born in a stable and placed in a feeding trough, the God who created the universe and everything in it fully reveals himself. It is truly an incredible claim to make and yet this is exactly what our faith proclaims.

Today's Gospel is hugely important because it serves to remind us that our priority must always be with Christ. Nothing can be more important than this revealed truth which must shape everything that we do. It is a profound mystery at one level but incredibly simple at another, that we have been granted access to the Father through his Son Jesus. Our starting point is with that stable in Bethlehem all those centuries ago when God made himself weak and vulnerable so that we might begin to understand the depth of his love for us. This is what we must be attracted to and fall in love with if we are ever going to understand anything about a God who is willing to do, literally, anything for us. Sometimes, we have to put all those unnecessary things to one side which prevent us from really seeing and experiencing God and return to the simplicity of Bethlehem because that is where we will find all we need to know about him.

I keep on using the word simple in this reflection and I am doing this quite deliberately. When we see and believe that Jesus is nothing less than the human face of God then that is the day when everything becomes clearer and yes, simpler. We can now return to the point where our reflection first started by saying that Jesus, in whom God is made flesh, is the one who comes in search of us, he comes to seek us out and he comes to find us. And why would he do this? Because he loves us with an unconditional love beyond anything we could ever imagine. If then we turn to him, what do we find? The answer of course is simple, the face of God himself.

*Something to think about or discuss:*

1. *Read the prologue to John's Gospel and identify the one most important claim and explain the reasons for your choice.*

2. *Why do you think the prologue to John's Gospel is read, in church, on Christmas day?*

3. *Do you see God as distant or close? Give reasons for your answer.*

4. *Is it right to describe the Christian faith as being simple? Can you explain why?*

5. *What does the prologue to John's Gospel encourage us to do in the practice of our faith?*

# Six:

## 'A Change of Heart'

Luke 2:22-40

## The Holy Family

*When the time came for their purification according to the law of Moses, they brought him up to Jerusalem to present him to the Lord (as it is written in the law of the Lord, "Every firstborn male shall be designated as holy to the Lord"), and they offered a sacrifice according to what is stated in the law of the Lord, "a pair of turtledoves or two young pigeons."*

*Now there was a man in Jerusalem whose name was Simeon; this man was righteous and devout, looking forward to the consolation of Israel, and the Holy Spirit rested on him. It had been revealed to him by the Holy Spirit that he would not see death before he had seen the Lord's Messiah. Guided by the Spirit, Simeon came into the temple; and when the parents brought in the child Jesus, to do for him what was customary under the law, Simeon took him in his arms and praised God, saying,*

*"Master, now you are dismissing your servant in peace, according to your word; for my eyes have seen your salvation, which you have prepared in the presence of all peoples, a light for revelation to the Gentiles and for glory to your people Israel."*

*And the child's father and mother were amazed at what was being said about him. Then Simeon blessed them and said to his mother Mary, "This child is destined for the falling and the rising of many in Israel, and to be a sign that will be opposed so that the inner thoughts of many will be revealed, and a sword will pierce your own soul too."*

*There was also a prophet, Anna the daughter of Phanuel, of the tribe of Asher. She was of a great age, having lived with her husband seven years after her marriage, then as a widow to the age of eighty-four. She never left the temple but worshiped there with fasting and prayer night and day. At that moment she came and began to praise God and to speak about the child to all who were looking for the redemption of Jerusalem.*

Today we are presented with a most beautiful and wonderful encounter between the Holy Family and Simeon who meet in the temple at the same time. Simeon, of course, has this great desire or hope in is heart that, one day, he will experience, personally, the consolation of God's people Israel. We are told that he is a *'righteous and devout man,'* on whom *'the Holy Spirit rested.'* At the same time, this, however, is no chance meeting because we are told that he is led by the Spirit and *'would not see death until he had seen the Christ of the Lord.'*

Let us recall that the Holy Family would appear to be, at least at first sight, just another ordinary family doing what was expected of them by the law. Yet, Simeon sees right through this to the moment he has been waiting for all his life by recognising the saviour of the world. He is overcome with joy and gently takes the child into his arms in a moment of remarkable intimacy. Perhaps, shaking with uncontrollable nerves he proceeds to bless both God and the family as we hear from his lips the quite beautiful words of the *Nunc Dimittis* through which he recognises the child as the saviour of humanity. This is the moment he has been waiting all his life for and now, at last, having seen it he can, *'go in peace.'* I would suggest that at this point we stay with this moment of intimacy and recognise that this is the way we should receive the Lord too, welcoming him into our hearts and our lives.

After this, however, there is a dramatic change in tone as Simeon approaches Mary. His message to her is one of great pain and sorrow when he tells her, *'A sword will pierce your soul.'* This is because the child, *'is destined for the fall and for the rise of many in Israel, destined to be a sign that is opposed.'* In this way Simeon is making it clear that some will reject the child as the Christ whilst others will accept him. Although he will be the light of the world, many will seek to extinguish his flame of unconditional love for all people. Many will have their lives transformed by him, whilst others will see him as a threat and seek his destruction. Hence, this child will be divisive, the people will either be for him or against him.

Perhaps, these thoughts are as true today as they ever were. To truly accept Jesus is, in fact, to undergo a change of heart. Remember what we said about conversion during Advent? Putting it another way, it could be said that our response to Jesus exposes what is in the depths of our own hearts. This in itself can be a painful process because it can take a lifetime to conform our lives, starting with our own hearts, to that of Jesus. Struggle, difficulty, and anguish are inevitable as we seek to uncover the unconditional love with which we, ourselves, are loved and to believe it with all sincerity. For this very reason we can take heart from the fact that struggle is a healthy part of the process, involving a radical transformation of life, as we respond to God's love as revealed to us in his Son, Jesus Christ.

This life-long conversion as a response to God's radical, life-transforming love brings with it a sense that the deeper we are drawn into the heart of God the more painful it becomes. Hence, Saint John of the Cross wrote about, *'The dark night of the soul,'* and Saint Mother Teresa, in the later years of her life, often reflected on the apparent absence of God in her prayer life. Perhaps, the closer we come to God, the more we experience the personal, intimate love of Christ, then the more we become aware of our own unworthiness. Again, this is a common feature of many of the lives of the saints. Yet it should not surprise us as we are drawn back to the meeting of Simeon with the Holy Family.

On this great feast day, we can now rest in the security of knowing that struggle is an inevitable part of our discipleship. This is because we are loved first. Loved by a God who, through his Son, is closer to us than we could ever imagine and loves us more than we can ever know. Or as Saint Paul put it, *'I can do everything through him who gives me strength.'* (Philippians 4:13)

*Something to think about or discuss:*

1. *Why do you think it is important for the church to celebrate the feast day of the Holy Family?*

2. *Write down three things you know now, which you did not know before reading this reflection?*

3. *In what ways, if any, has this reflection helped you understand your own relationship with God better?*

4. *What role does struggle play in your own life of faith? Is such struggle good or bad? Try to give reasons for your answer.*

5. *What is the Good News to be found in this reflection? How might you go about sharing it with others?*

**Seven:**

## 'Mary: Mother of Jesus and Our Mother Too'

Luke 2:16-21

## Mary, Mother of God

*So, they went with haste and found Mary and Joseph, and the child lying in the manger. When they saw this, they made known what had been told them about this child; and all who heard it were amazed at what the shepherds told them. But Mary treasured all these words and pondered them in her heart. The shepherds returned, glorifying, and praising God for all they had heard and seen, as it had been told them.*

*After eight days had passed, it was time to circumcise the child; and he was called Jesus, the name given by the angel before he was conceived in the womb.*

Over the years several friends and colleagues, who were not Catholic, have pointed out to me why they are not comfortable with the way in which the church relates to Mary mother of Jesus. I thought I would begin this reflection by sharing some of them with you. Many have pointed out that the church seems to idealise Mary in an unhealthy way. Thus, by highlighting Mary as a perpetual virgin who remained chaste and pure after conceiving and giving birth to Jesus, presents the danger of comparing all women to her. How is it possible, they argue, to live up to such an idealised image? Hence, the result is that *'ordinary'* women are treated, at the very least, with disrespect by a church dominated and controlled by men. In this way stereotypes are created which make it impossible for those women who cannot live up to such expectations to thrive. The result is rampant sexism and a male-controlled church.

Another charge is that Mary is treated by Catholics like God. She is given a number of titles and assigned what might be called a protective role. Here, Mary the perfect women, now also becomes the perfect mother, who takes charge of her children by guarding and protecting them from all forms of evil. Those who adopt this line of thinking then go on to make the point that it appears Mary has either replaced God or at least acquired equal status with him. Furthermore, those who hold such beliefs have been fed a diet of immature faith, which seeks to control and dominate a naïve and uneducated laity.

Is any of this true? Here, I must be honest enough to admit that at least some of it might be and that it is important to reflect on and learn from what others might say to us about Mary. However, very often it has been my experience that many people have a distorted understanding of Mary in the life of the Catholic Church based on false perceptions. So now I would like to present, on this solemnity dedicated to her, the way in which Mary is both understood and loved by Catholics.

First and foremost, devotion to Mary as the Mother of Jesus and therefore as the Mother of God places the feminine at the very heart of our faith. It seems obvious to say but God chose this woman, above all other women to be the mother of his Son. The incarnation, therefore, starts with a woman, who using her own free will, agreed to conceive the Son of God in her womb. There can be no greater honour placed on a human being than that. Mary, the woman, on behalf of humanity says, *'yes'* to God and so the story of our salvation begins. In this way, we are encouraged to follow the example of Mary, because it always leads to God.

I would also, at this point, argue that we need to stay with the feminine and, perhaps, going against much of what popular culture maintains, suggest that it has certain unique characteristics, which helps define our humanity. Or putting it another way, in the female you can often find concentrated those aspects of our humanity, which Jesus often highlighted as revelations of God. Here, I am talking about tenderness, gentleness, intimacy, compassion, and love. The very process of carrying a child in the womb, for nine months, before finally giving birth shapes a woman into how she perceives and relates to the world. All of this points to and serves to highlight just how important Mary is in the life of the church but in the same way it also makes abundantly clear the vital role all women must play in its life if it is to be an authentic witness to God who, himself, chose Mary to give birth to his Son. After all no man could ever have occupied such a privileged status.

For all these reasons, I would say that the church needs the feminine and that Mary encapsulates and points to, what this really means. When we lose sight of this, we are in danger of betraying a precious gift given to us by God himself, so we must always keep in mind, that which is said to us by those looking from what appears to be the outside. In its purist form devotion to Mary will always lead us to her Son, Jesus, whilst at the same time reminding us of the need to value the role of the feminine in the life of the church. In this Christmas season I find it most helpful to reflect on Mary, as a loving mother, holding Jesus tenderly in her arms. Yet at the same time, Jesus offers himself to us from the warm embrace of his mother. What an image this is of humanity and divinity bound in love to each other. In my parish church of Our Lady of the Wayside, Shirley, there stands a life size statue of Mary and Jesus, carved out of a single block of wood. The child clings to his mother as she holds him gently in her arms neither wanting to let the other go. Personally, I find power in such an image because it reveals perfectly through mother and child how God feels about us. Holding us, embracing us, loving us, and never wanting to let us go, just how a mother feels about her child.

Today, in this Christmas season, is a solemnity dedicated to Mary as the Mother of God. At the same time, it is the start of a New Year, so what can we hope for and what can we learn from our reflection on Mary? Perhaps, we can draw strength from her faithfulness and her surrender to God's will. After all, when this small insignificant young lady said, '*yes*' to God, her life was to change forever and would never be the same again. Ultimately, she became a disciple of her own son and followed him wherever he went. This took her to the foot of the cross where he was crucified, to the tomb in which he was buried and finally to the upper room where the Holy Spirit was poured out on her at Pentecost. Mary did all of this because she was a mother, a mother to a son, who was the saviour of the world. This is what mothers do, serve and love. It is for this reason that Catholics refer to Mary as the Mother of the Church and I am proud and honoured to call Mary my Mother too.

*Something to think about or discuss:*

1. *Can you think of ways people often misunderstand the role of Mary in the life of the church today?*

2. *What role, if any, does Mary play in your own life of faith?*

3. *Do you think it is important that the church dedicates a day to Mary such as, 'The Solemnity of Mary Mother of God'?*
   *Try to give reasons for your answer.*

4. *Do you think the role of women is recognised enough in the life of the church today? What can or should be done about it?*

5. *Do you find yourself agreeing or disagreeing with what the reflection says about the feminine in the life of the church?*
   *Try to give reasons for your answer.*

# Eight:

## 'Letting Go'

Matthew 2:1-12

## The Epiphany

*In the time of King Herod, after Jesus was born in Bethlehem of Judea, wise men from the East came to Jerusalem, asking, "Where is the child who has been born king of the Jews? For we observed his star at its rising and have come to pay him homage." When King Herod heard this, he was frightened, and all Jerusalem with him; and calling together all the chief priests and scribes of the people, he inquired of them where the Messiah was to be born. They told him, "In Bethlehem of Judea; for so it has been written by the prophet: 'And you, Bethlehem, in the land of Judah, are by no means least among the rulers of Judah; for from you shall come a ruler who is to shepherd my people, Israel.'"*

*Then Herod secretly called for the wise men and learned from them the exact time when the star had appeared. Then he sent them to Bethlehem, saying, "Go and search diligently for the child; and when you have found him, bring me word so that I may also go and pay him homage." When they had heard the king, they set out; and there, ahead of them, went the star that they had seen at its rising, until it stopped over the place where the child was. When they saw that the star had stopped, they were overwhelmed with joy. On entering the house, they saw the child with Mary his mother; and they knelt down and paid him homage. Then, opening their treasure chests, they offered him gifts of gold, frankincense, and myrrh. And having been warned in a dream not to return to Herod, they left for their own country by another road.*

Letting go is never easy. So, as we arrive at the Epiphany, I find myself asking the question, *what do we have to let go of, if we are to truly discover the reality of God?* Equally, is it our reluctance to let go of what we hold most dear, which prevents us from recognising God at all? These are challenging questions but very often, and as we have seen, this is what the Gospel does. Taking it a stage further, how resistant are we to letting go? Indeed, and as we have already said, what is that we must let go of? Finally, perhaps, we need to think about what threatens us the most and how we react when the challenge to really discover God comes our way.

Why was Jesus so very often rejected and treated with hostility by the political and religious leaders of his day? Perhaps, it was because they saw him as a threat to their privileged status. When this happened, they became blind to the reality of who Jesus was failing to recognise him as the Son of God. Putting it another way, they ultimately refused to let go of their power, wealth, and status. We must guard against falling into such a trap, ourselves, lest we either fail to recognise God or rather turn him into something we want him to be which no longer threatens us. Let us see now what happens when we apply this way of thinking to the Epiphany.

The first thing to note, is that the Magi come from the East a place associated with paganism and knowledge. That area of the world had a reputation for science and learning, which included astrology. It is not beyond the realms of possibility that the Magi had been studying the mystery of the heavens all their lives before discovering something which they believed had huge significance for the whole world. For them, perhaps, a great truth was about to be revealed that would change the course of human history forever. Seeing the sign for this in the skies they now had to let go of everything they knew and were familiar with, to pursue an invitation they simply could not resist. Where it would lead them, they did not know, but it was something they knew, had to be done.

What an exotic sight they must have been as they entered Jerusalem in search not just of a king but of the King of all Kings. Their objective was a simple one, to find this new king and worship him. Yet, they needed help. Certain that neither Herod nor Caesar Augustus were the kings they were looking for, the Magi admitted that their own knowledge needed help. Once again, they had to let go of their own pride to seek aid in their quest. As far as King Herod is concerned, he and he alone is the only legitimate King of the Jews. It is for this reason that he recognises the threat posed by the Magi and their claims. Hence, Herod cannot see beyond his own power, wealth, and status, refusing to admit, even the possibility, that something new is happening right before his very eyes. No, for him, the threat must be eliminated, by any means necessary, if he is to preserve his own privileged position given to him by Rome. Here we see directly, in action, what we identified at the start of our reflection, as to how a threat to our accepted view of the world can prevent us from encountering the reality of God. Compare this to the Magi who have let go of everything, to undergo a journey, in search of the truth. Is this a price we are prepared to pay too?

The Magi, however, continue on their way in search of a greater truth. Before them is the star, the great sign in the sky leading them ever forward. As we know, their journey is not easy, at times they lose their way but there is something stronger within them, a purpose which will not let them give up. Inspired by the belief that what they are doing is more important than anything else, they push on, leaving their former lives behind, rejecting comfort for something far greater, the truth. Then finally, they reach the stable and find the child they have been searching for all their lives lying in a manger. Now these three Magi, wise men, or kings from the East fall on their knees and worship him. What a strange sight this must have been for Mary and Joseph, yet there was still more to come. For the Magi Jesus was, in fact, their king above all others. In recognising him as such they then let go of all they had, their most valuable possessions, laying them before him to be used as he thinks fit. Nothing now, therefore, shall come between them and this King of all Kings, for in him they have found that which they have been searching for their whole lives, the truth. In this symbolic act of worship and adoration the Magi are offering Jesus their whole lives, everything they are, and everything they have, holding nothing back. In other words, it is a total letting go. Only then does true recognition take place.

Now we need to come back to ourselves and our own lives of faith today. Are we like the Magi kneeling before the Lord offering him everything we have, or do we always find ourselves holding something back? Can we admit to ourselves that, perhaps, the doubt in the back of our mind is that which prevents us from truly knowing God? That, in all honesty, we have always held something back from him because we feel too vulnerable to do anything else. Yet the invitation remains the same and it will never change. Come to the stable, look into the manger and see the Christ child. Fall to your knees and worship him, offering him everything and holding nothing back. When life seems hard and dark, and when you stumble and fall, which we all do, look again for the star to guide your way because it is always there. Take heart from the fact that with God we can always begin again, because he is the God of second chances, and third and fourth and so on. Until, eventually, we reach that moment in our own lives, whereby, just like those Magi who saw and believed, that letting go of everything, leads ultimately, in fact, to finding the truth.

*Something to think about or discuss:*

1. *Can you think of a time in your life when you had to let go of something really important to you? How did you feel?*

2. *What do you think God invites us to let go of, if we are to truly find him? Try to explain your answer.*

3. *Why do you think many people find it difficult to find or believe in God today? Can you suggest possible reasons for your answer?*

4. *How might the story of the Magi inspire us in our journey of faith today?*

5. *What do you think is meant by, 'letting go of everything to find God'? Is this even possible?*

**Nine:**

## 'Send Forth Your Spirit, O Lord, and Renew the Face of The Earth'

Mark 1:7-11

### The Baptism of Jesus

*He proclaimed, "The one who is more powerful than I is coming after me; I am not worthy to stoop down and untie the thong of his sandals. I have baptized you with water; but he will baptize you with the Holy Spirit."*

*In those days Jesus came from Nazareth of Galilee and was baptized by John in the Jordan. And just as he was coming up out of the water, he saw the heavens torn apart and the Spirit descending like a dove on him. And a voice came from heaven, "You are my Son, the Beloved; with you I am well pleased.*

As we come to the end of the Christmas season, marked by the Baptism of Jesus, it gives us the opportunity to reflect on the Holy Spirit. When we think about it, therefore, how dependant are we on the Holy Spirit? In the Gospel reading for today John the Baptist says, *'I baptise you with water, but he will baptise you with the Holy Spirit.'* How many of us, though, spend any time reflecting on our own baptism? How many of us reflect on the fact that through the sacrament of baptism it is Christ himself who baptises us and it is through him that the Holy Spirit is poured out and into our lives? As a result, baptism not only makes us members of his body on earth, the church, but also it is the sacrament through which Christ shares his very life with us, a life which is eternal. Yet despite this, we tend to forget the role of the Holy Spirit. Every time a Catholic enters a church we dip our fingers in holy water and make the sign of the cross on our own bodies to remind ourselves of our baptism. In death the coffin is sprinkled with holy water to remind us, once again, of our baptism and the gift of eternal life bestowed upon us by Christ. However, throughout our lives of faith, whatever form this may take, we tend to forget the Holy Spirit. As today we celebrate the baptism of Jesus, we are given the opportunity to reflect on the crucial role of the Holy Spirit both in our own lives, and in that of the church.

The start of a New Year provides us with the ideal opportunity to go back to the Holy Spirit and rediscover a gift, given to us by God, which is beyond price. The Book of Revelation, the last book in the Bible, was written in a time of great persecution for the church and yet one refrain stands out above all others, '*Let anyone who can hear, listen to what the Spirit is saying to the churches.*' What then might the Spirit be saying to us today? Perhaps, the crucial starting point to this question is to ask another one, '*how are we receiving the Spirit in our own lives today?*' But let us begin, however, with a further question, '*how do we see the Spirit and what do we expect from it?*' The words of Psalm 103 help us out here when it implores, '*Send Forth Your Spirit, O Lord, and Renew the Face of the Earth.*' You see the Holy Spirit is all about creation. Remember the book of Genesis where we are told how the Holy Spirit hovered over the waters? Or how at Pentecost the Holy Spirit transformed the hearts and minds of the Apostles in the upper room? Sometimes we just have to turn to the Holy Spirit and ask for our own minds and hearts to be changed. Ultimately, we can do nothing without God, and very often we all make the mistake of thinking we can do everything by ourselves. Little wonder, therefore, that the tasks appear to be too big and the obstacles too daunting. When this happens and we are tempted to give in, the real problem is our refusal to be dependent on the Holy Spirit. Now fear rules our hearts and our minds as we see ourselves surrounded by darkness.

At this point, we need to change, and our attitude to life and faith needs to be transformed. The solution is, in fact, right there before our very eyes and it has been there all along because the answer lies in Christ. We must open our minds, our hearts, and our very souls to the Holy Spirit, allowing him to work on us. Going back to the day we were baptised, our parents and God parents make a decision on our behalf, which is to give us to Christ. Hence, our lives belong to him, but how often do we forget the fact that we live our lives constantly in his embrace?

The solution to everything then always involves turning our lives over to him, who is closer to us than we could ever imagine and loves us more than we could ever know. Saint Paul discovered this for himself when he came to the conclusion that he must model his life on that of Jesus until, *it was no longer, he who lived but Christ who lived in him.*

Once we begin to understand this, and it may take a lifetime, we come to a remarkable conclusion. That the Spirit of Jesus, remember he baptised us, shared his life with us and we are part of his body on earth the church, lives on in our minds and hearts today. In fact, that is what a life of faith actually means, a calling to be so dependent on the Holy Spirit, that we are living the life of Christ now. What a privilege and responsibility that is, not only to bring the life of Christ to others but to recognise him in everyone we meet. Yet none of this is possible without the Holy Spirit. However, this is true not only of our own lives of faith but of the church too. Filled with the Grace of the Holy Spirit the church, as the body of Christ, is called to live its life for others and that includes all people. To be a light to the nations and a sign of hope for the world.

Very often we are tempted to be overwhelmed by the crisis which many people claim the church faces today. Lack of vocations, falling attendances, and rival factions can often deflect us from a deeper and more important truth, that Christ will never abandon his people. Instead, what is needed is the strength of faith to see something else that, perhaps, is taking place, as it always has done, right before our very eyes, a recreation. All we need to do, in response to this, is to place all our hope and all our trust in God, and to remember the words of Revelation, *'Let anyone who can hear, listen to what the Spirit is saying to the churches.'* The important lesson to learn here, therefore, is to simply allow God's will to be done and not ours. Jesus, himself, baptised us with his Holy Spirit, the same Spirit which created the world and everything in it, and the same Spirit which was poured out on the Apostles at Pentecost. This means that at the start of this New Year, we can now turn with complete confidence in God, our heavenly Father, and ask him to, *'Send Forth Your Spirit, O Lord, and Renew the Face of the Earth'.*

*Something to think about or discuss:*

1. *What does the Holy Spirit mean to you?*

2. *Why is baptism so important in our life of faith?*

3. *What difficult challenges does the church face today?*

4. *How can the church be a light to the nations in the modern world and a symbol of hope for humanity?*

5. *How would you like to the church change if it is to be true to its mission of proclaiming the Gospel of Jesus Christ?*

# Year C:

# Luke

*He said to them, "Why were you searching for me? Did you not know that I must be in my Father's house?" But they did not understand what he said to them. Then he went down with them and came to Nazareth and was obedient to them. His mother treasured all these things in her heart. (Luke 2:49-51)*

# Luke and Advent

As we journey through Advent with Luke we are confronted with several challenges. The first one, is to wake up, to open our eyes, and be completely honest with ourselves about what is going on in our lives of faith today. All too often we fall into the trap of either doing nothing or leaving it all up to God. Well Advent provides us with the opportunity to begin again. For some people life becomes routine whilst for others life is hard, harsh, and cruel. The early Christians were faced with the same issues and were told to, *'Lift up your heads.'* Perhaps, this year, therefore, we could examine our own lives of faith starting with the route to our hearts.

John the Baptist strikes us as an uncompromising figure, and his message demands a conversion of the heart, if we are to truly recognise Jesus. To do this, we must be totally honest with ourselves by recognising all those things which have to be cleared out, if we are to let God in. Hence, during Advent we need to give ourselves time with the Lord, allowing the grace of the Holy Spirit to get to work on our lives. This, however, has and always will be a two-way process, whereby God invites, and we respond. So, what might God be asking us to do this Advent?

On the Third week of Advent, we will come across the challenge, *'Actions Speak Louder than Words.'* This is really important as it gives us the opportunity to commit ourselves to something but what will that be? Christianity is not a passive religion but invites its followers to conform their lives to that of Christ, and this is impossible without doing something because doing nothing is not an option. How then, might our lives of faith change this Advent, and how will this be reflected in what we do?

Finally, we focus our attention on Mary and what she reveals about discipleship today. Mary of course, teaches us to listen to God, to place all our hope and all our trust in him, to rejoice, and then to spend the rest of our lives bringing Jesus to others, through our lives of faith.

# One:

## 'Stand Up and be Counted'

Luke 21:25-28, 34-36

## First Sunday of Advent

*"There will be signs in the sun, the moon, and the stars, and on the earth distress among nations confused by the roaring of the sea and the waves. People will faint from fear and foreboding of what is coming upon the world, for the powers of the heavens will be shaken. Then they will see 'the Son of Man coming in a cloud' with power and great glory. Now when these things begin to take place, stand up and raise your heads, because your redemption is drawing near."*

*"Be on guard so that your hearts are not weighed down with dissipation and drunkenness and the worries of this life, and that day does not catch you unexpectedly, like a trap. For it will come upon all who live on the face of the whole earth. Be alert at all times, praying that you may have the strength to escape all these things that will take place, and to stand before the Son of Man."*

As we enter the season of Advent and so begin our preparations for the celebration of Our Lord's birth at Christmas, pause and take a moment to look around you, watch the evening news and observe what is going on in the world. What do you see? War, terrorism, poverty, famine, inequality, sexism, racism, and destruction of the planet to name but a few. Now, how does this make you feel? Depressed, inadequate, and helpless, perhaps? So, what can you do, given the scale of such issues? To help us answer this question it might be helpful to go back and examine the context of our Gospel reading for today.

Our early brothers and sisters, in Christ, were surrounded by hostility. The fledging church found itself at the very heart of one of the most powerful empires the world has ever known, Rome. Persecution of the faith was commonplace as it became outlawed by the emperor. Indeed, Christianity was viewed as an enemy of Rome and, as such, its followers were identified as traitors and, as a result, were liable to arrest, torture and execution. It was under such circumstances that those early Christians turned their thoughts to the return of Jesus. It is against such a background that we find the opening warnings in the Gospel reading for today. Little wonder then that the early church feared for its very life. Yet what were they to do?

Jesus himself tells them, *'Stand up and lift up your heads. Be always on the watch and pray.'* Or in other words have faith. The words of Jesus, however, are not only timeless but are also the words life. Hence, for this reason, they are addressed directly to us as his followers today. Once again, we, as a church, find ourselves surrounded by all kinds of difficulties and challenges, which often threaten to overwhelm us but what are we to do? First and foremost, let us return to sacred scripture and listen again, with the ears of faith, to what Jesus is actually saying to us. *'Lift up your heads,'* exhorts Jesus and be people who are positive and confident. Turn to one another and offer words of support and encouragement. Pope Francis often talks about Christianity as being a religion of joy but where, in truth, has all the joy gone? All too often our faith is consumed by the problems which threaten and surround us and yet Jesus has come to liberate us, and therefore, to set us free. Hence, we need to encourage each other and not be despondent.

However, it is true that for many people life is hard and can be so terribly cruel. When this happens, the danger is that our hearts become hardened, and our attitudes based on closed minds. On the other hand, for some people, life becomes comfortable leading to indifference to the suffering of others. As a result, and without realising it, something creeps up on us, which has the effect of dehumanising us. When this happens, we stop listening to the words of life given to us by Jesus and their impact on our lives of faith become negligible. It is for this reason that we are always told to, *'Stay awake, and be on the alert and to lift up your heads.'* Yet, how many of us skim over the Gospel reading, failing to allow the word of God to impact directly on our lives? Today Jesus invites us to, *'Pray that you may be able to escape all that is about to happen to you.'*

Ultimately what we find in today's Gospel reading is a challenge to recognise the presence of the risen Lord in our midst, inviting us to turn to him as the source of life itself. Can we recognise him in the readings, in the Eucharist, and in each other? Can we wake up, open our eyes, and see what is right there before us? Perhaps, the starting point is to pray for the strength to recognise Christ in our own lives so that we might learn to, *'Stand before the Son of Man,'* and so follow him with our whole being. Our early brothers and sisters, all those centuries ago, in that fledgling church learnt a valuable lesson, which in turn, they passed on to us. Above all else, place all your hope and all your trust in God, then despite whatever happens, he will always strengthen and sustain you to face the trials and tribulations which will come your way. Such trust, hope and faith make us not only more human but also more like Christ and this is true not only of our individual lives of faith but also of the church too. For this is what the world desperately needs today, a church which is not only a light to the nations but a source of hope for the whole of humanity.

*Something to think about or discuss:*

1. *What worries you most about the state of the world today?*

2. *What do you think Jesus means by, 'Stand up and lift up your heads?'*

3. *How would you describe your own prayer life?*

4. *How difficult is it to live a life of Christian joy?*

5. *Do you think the church, today, is a light to the nations and a source of hope for people?*

# Two:

## 'Preparing our Hearts'

Luke 3:1-6

## Second Sunday of Advent

*In the fifteenth year of the reign of Emperor Tiberius, when Pontius Pilate was governor of Judea, and Herod was ruler of Galilee, and his brother Philip ruler of the region of Ituraea and Trachonitis, and Lysanias ruler of Abilene, during the high priesthood of Annas and Caiaphas, the word of God came to John son of Zechariah in the wilderness. He went into all the region around the Jordan, proclaiming a baptism of repentance for the forgiveness of sins, as it is written in the book of the words of the prophet Isaiah, "The voice of one crying out in the wilderness: 'Prepare the way of the Lord, make his paths straight. Every valley shall be filled, and every mountain and hill shall be made low, and the crooked shall be made straight, and the rough ways made smooth; and all flesh shall see the salvation of God.'"*

One of the things which has hit me most, over the years, about reflecting on the Gospels is the way in which God reveals himself. Indeed, I would go as far as to say, that there is a pattern to the way in which God's grace works in the world and this becomes more than obvious in today's reading. Here I am talking about the way in which God appears to reject the rich and powerful in order to express his will. Luke understands this as he spends so much time setting the scene for the arrival of John the Baptist. Note how he names the emperor, Tiberius Caesar, and the year of his reign. In the same way, he is specific about the governor of Judea, Pontius Pilate, Herod the tetrarch of Galilee and even names his brother Philip as the tetrarch of Ituraea and Trachonitis. As if that was not enough, he goes on to mention Lysanias as tetrarch of Abilene and the fact that Annas and Caiaphas hold the office of the high priesthood. Yet God does not reveal his will through any of these, instead Luke interrupts his list of the rich and powerful in a stark and blunt way when he tells us, *'The word of God came to John in the desert.'* Putting it another way, the rich and powerful of the world have no control over God's grace. Indeed, as far as we know, they are completely oblivious to what is about to take place. This is a sobering message, on this Second Sunday of Advent, to all of us who would attempt to discern God's will. The most powerful man on earth, the emperor, in charge of one of the most powerful empires the world has ever known, is totally ignorant of God's grace, at work, in the world. Indeed, even the high priest responsible for the temple in Jerusalem, the very place where God dwelt with his people knows nothing of God's intentions.

Now we can come to John, alone, in the wilderness. Here is the place where God's chosen instrument will have to depend totally on Him if he is to survive. There are no trappings of luxury for John. Rather the prophet has to learn what is essential to live. Contrast this with the lifestyles of the emperor in his palace in Rome or that of King Herod. Later we will learn that John dressed in camel skin, eating wild locusts and honey. Yet, his life was filled by God, and it was for Him that he lived. John learnt in that wild place what was essential to live, and his heart burned with a love, which consumed him. In this way the prophet could put down deep roots into the source of his very reason for existing and feed on that constantly. Putting that which was not essential to one side John recognised what was really needed to live, God, and for him this changed everything. His understanding of life and God was now transformed, and if others were to see this too then a conversion was needed, which called for baptism. As a result, when John invited the people to him on the banks of the river Jordan, he challenged them to begin life again. If the people were to truly recognise the one who was coming, then they must reject their old way of living and embrace something new. All that they clung to, which prevented their eyes from being opened, must now be rejected. This was not only a defining moment in their own lives but in the history of humanity. Such was the power of John's message. At this moment, perhaps, we should stop and reflect on the huge difference between John as he stood, dressed in camel skin, in the wilderness, on the banks of the river Jordan, with that of

Caiaphas in the palace of the high priest in Jerusalem, and the palatial setting of the emperor surrounded by luxury in Rome.

How then can we now apply this to our own lives of faith today? John points us in the right direction when he draws on the prophet Isaiah and urges us to, *'Prepare the way of the Lord.'* This means opening our hearts to the God of love, who always makes the first move in searching for us, but we must be honest enough with ourselves to recognise what prevents this from happening. After all, it is far easier to have hard hearts and closed minds. The simple truth is that God is closer to us than we could ever imagine and loves us more than we could ever know. Yet what stops us from realising this? By closing our minds and hardening our hearts we make it more difficult for God to reach us. So, what must we do on this Second Sunday of Advent to let God in? Perhaps, the first thing we need to do is to clear a pathway to our own hearts and to achieve this something radical is required. John the Baptist made this very clear to the people who flocked to him, in the wilderness, by telling them that they had to make a choice between God and all that which stood in the way of him reaching their hearts. In other words, conversion was essential if they were ever to recognise the one who would come after him. Hence, the first thing we need to do, is recognise that our own *conversion* is essential, and this requires a complete change of heart. After this, we need to be able to identify all those things, in our lives, which prevent God from reaching our hearts and clear them out. Think here of the opening words of our Gospel for today and why God chose John the Baptist. Now produce a list of your own priorities and identify the essential from the none-essential. Is it possible to let go of all those luxuries in life which block the pathway to our hearts? Going deeper into our lives, is it possible to identify the crooked pathways we have been heading down and change direction before it is too late? Can we revisit our own baptism and reflect on the enormity of what it means and do the same for our children? Is it possible to look at our membership of the church and honestly reflect on our own commitment to its mission?

This, of course, is all challenging stuff but it is meant to be. It is impossible to be half-hearted followers of Christ and part of the problem is that we have convinced ourselves that it is. Advent serves to remind us that now is the time for change, and now is the time to prepare our own hearts for what is to come. Stay for a while then with John the Baptist and listen again to his message of conversion but be prepared to apply it to your own life because God stands at the door of our hearts even now, but the question still remains, will we let him in?

*Something to think about or discuss:*

1. *Why do you think God chooses to act in ways we least expect? Can you think of examples?*

2. *Why do you think Luke spends so much time listing dates and characters at the start of the Gospel reading for today? Is this important? Can you give reasons for your answer?*

3. *Can you summarise the message of John the Baptist for people today?*

4. *Why, do you think, so many people came to John in the desert?*

5. *What must we do, in our lives of faith, in response to the message of John the Baptist?*

# Three:

## 'Actions Speak Louder than Words'

Luke 3:10-18

## Third Sunday of Advent

*And the crowds asked him, "What then should we do?" In reply he said to them, "Whoever has two coats must share with anyone who has none; and whoever has food must do likewise." Even tax collectors came to be baptized, and they asked him, "Teacher, what should we do?" He said to them, "Collect no more than the amount prescribed for you." Soldiers also asked him, "And we, what should we do?" He said to them, "Do not extort money from anyone by threats or false accusation and be satisfied with your wages."*

*As the people were filled with expectation, and all were questioning in their hearts concerning John, whether he might be the Messiah, John answered all of them by saying, "I baptize you with water; but one who is more powerful than I is coming; I am not worthy to untie the thong of his sandals. He will baptize you with the Holy Spirit and fire. His winnowing fork is in his hand, to clear his threshing floor and to gather the wheat into his granary; but the chaff he will burn with unquenchable fire."*

*So, with many other exhortations, he proclaimed the good news to the people.*

Today's reading is a continuation of where we were last week only now, we are one step closer to celebrating the birth of Our Lord and Saviour at Christmas. As we saw last time, the people were drawn to John the Baptist in large numbers, as they heeded his warning to be converted. John spoke directly to their hearts and, in effect, was inviting them to return to lives which were more authentic witnesses to their faith in God. In response the people cried out, *'what shall we do?'* John's response is simple and direct. How you live your life day to day, matters. How you treat each other, especially those less fortunate than yourselves, matters. How your heart responds to the cries of the poor which surround you, matters. The feelings which lie deep in your hearts about right and wrong, matters. How you relate to and live with each other, matters. In other words, John was inviting the people to react and respond to his challenge of not only what it means to believe in God, but equally, what it means to be human. In this respect, what was needed, therefore, was action because actions always speak louder than words.

John, in fact, makes things very simple, whilst challenging people to accept responsibility for themselves and each other, when he says, *'The man who has two tunics should share with him who has none, and the one who has food should do the same.'* How do we respond to this today on the Third Sunday of Advent? Perhaps, first and foremost, we must be honest with ourselves and, once again, turn to our own hearts. In the previous reflection we were invited to think about all those things in life which prevented God from finding the pathway to our hearts. Now we must be more concrete in doing this, by accepting the challenge given to us by John the Baptist. So, let us begin, by thinking about all those people across the world today who live in poverty:

- 6.5 billion people – 85% of the world's population – live in developing countries

- 1.3 billion people – live in absolute poverty and over half of them are children

- 844 million people – do not have access to clean drinking water

- 1 in 3 people – do not have access to a toilet

- 1 in 13 children die before the age of 5 in Sub-Saharan Africa

- 1 in 143 children die before the age of 5 in wealthy nations

- 1 in ten people - live on less than £1.48 a day

Such statistics are both frightening and challenging but in response spend a moment or two reflecting on the contents of your own wardrobe and fridge. Then think about the difference between what we need and what we want:

- Around 9 million people die every year of hunger and hunger related diseases. This is more than AIDS, malaria and tuberculosis combined.

- A child dies every 10 seconds from hunger

- 3.1 million children die every year, under the age of 5, from poor nutrition and hunger

- 822 million people suffer from undernourishment

- 1 in 9 people go to bed hungry every night

- 113 million people suffer from acute hunger meaning they are in urgent need of food and nutrients

John the Baptist told the people what they must do if they were to recognise God. The danger for us is that we have clogged up the pathway to our hearts with so much wealth and luxury that God cannot find a way through. Yet, it is never too late to undergo a conversion. The first step in this process is to open up our minds and our hearts to the working of the Holy Spirit and to be aware of what is going on in the world around us. To hear the cries of the poor, and to realise that we have been living as slaves for too long. Slaves to our own comfortable lifestyles and wealth. Putting it another way, by stopping our ears and looking away we have, in effect, dehumanised ourselves. Now, is the time to stop, and recognise the God who cries out to us in all those who suffer and do something about it. All too soon, we will see the child born in stable and lying in a manger whilst forgetting his birth is one in solidarity with all those who are poor. Pope Francis continues to call for a church which has a preferential option for the poor. Well now is the time to do something about it.

So, for a moment, forget all that infighting which threatens to pull the church of Christ in multiple directions, and instead focus on what John the Baptist invites us to do, if we are to truly recognise the God whose birth we are about to celebrate. Our hearts need to focus on mercy, compassion, forgiveness, justice, and love. Each of us needs to reflect on the invitation to change direction, clear a pathway to our hearts and free ourselves from the captivity which has held us back for so long. After all, actions do speak louder than words, and when the people asked John, '*What should we do then?*' He replied, '*The man with two tunics should share with him who has none, and the one who has food should do the same.*' It is over to us now.

*Something to think about or discuss:*

1. *How does the data presented in this reflection make you feel?*

2. *How can we be said to be living our lives in captivity today?*

3. *What can we do in response to John the Baptist's challenge in today's Gospel?*

4. *What kind of church do you want to be a member of?*

5. *Pope Francis calls for the church to have, 'a preferential option for the poor?' What does this mean and how is it linked to the preaching of John the Baptist?*

# Four:

## 'Mary Shows us the Way'

Luke 1:39-45

## Fourth Sunday of Advent

*In those days Mary set out and went with haste to a Judean town in the hill country, where she entered the house of Zechariah and greeted Elizabeth. When Elizabeth heard Mary's greeting, the child leaped in her womb. And Elizabeth was filled with the Holy Spirit and exclaimed with a loud cry, "Blessed are you among women, and blessed is the fruit of your womb. And why has this happened to me that the mother of my Lord comes to me? For as soon as I heard the sound of your greeting, the child in my womb leaped for joy. And blessed is she who believed that there would be a fulfilment of what was spoken to her by the Lord."*

We have concentrated our thoughts on John the Baptist for the last two weeks, Luke now connects the prophet's birth with that of Jesus. However, what is quite remarkable about today's Gospel reading is that no men are present. Zacharias, the father of John has, as we know, been struck dumb and Joseph is nowhere to be seen. Instead, what we are left with are two mothers. Each of them in their own unique way have been invited by God to co-operate with him, in his plan, for the salvation of the whole world. Such is the scene created by Luke. We should not be surprised, however, that it is the exclusive role of women that we are being invited to reflect upon here. The fact that, to some it is, becomes a damning indictment on our church today and a shameful thing for me to have to admit. Yet, scripture sets the record straight and, if we listen, will always point us in the right direction.

In this reflection we will now concentrate our thoughts on Mary and the relationship she has with her son, Jesus. So, right from the start there is a sense of urgency to the story as we are told, *'Mary got ready and hurried to a town in the hill country of Judea.'* Despite the layers of titles which have been applied to Mary over the centuries and the various devotions attached to her, what we have here is the tale of a simple mother. We can imagine her beaming with enthusiasm and excitement as she makes her way to Elizabeth. On her arrival something quite remarkable happens which Luke wants us to rejoice with too. Elizabeth filled with the Holy Spirit cannot contain herself when she cries out, *'Blessed are you among women, and blessed is the child you will bear! But why am I so favoured, that the mother of my Lord should come to me?'* Here we can see the close link between Mary and Jesus, because above and beyond any other title given to her, she is the mother of the Lord. This, in fact, is what Luke wants us to see and believe too, as we are invited to join in with Elizabeth's acclamation. For this reason, Mary and Jesus are inseparable from each other and this is why she is, *'Blessed among women and blessed is the fruit of her womb.'* Right from the very start, therefore, we can clearly see in the Gospel of Luke, that Mary gives us her son, Jesus.'

What else though does Elizabeth see in Mary that we are invited to share in too? The answer is, of course, complete trust in God or in other words, faith. Hence, Elizabeth declares, *'Blessed is she who has believed that what the Lord has said to her will be accomplished.'* In other words, Mary does not just agree to give birth to the Son of God, as great as that is, but listened and said, *'yes'* to her Lord. In the foothills of Galilee, in a small obscure village called Nazareth, a young unknown, and quite unremarkable women, heard an invitation from God to co-operate with his plan for the salvation of the world. Her response, no matter the cost, was to agree, and from that point on her life was to change for ever. Here we learn how Mary knew how to listen to, and trust in the word of God. Indeed, we are also told how Mary kept all these things in her heart where she would have constantly reflected on what it all meant. Above all, we can say that Mary was a woman of faith. Not just because she agreed to co-operate with God but that this made demands on her, the like of which, it is hard for us to even imagine. Yet the one precious thing we can take from Mary today is that she trusted and believed in God, above all things. Or putting it another way she was a woman of faith. We would do well on this Fourth Sunday of Advent to follow her example.

Armed with faith, then, Mary sets off on this journey to Elizabeth taking Jesus with her. The important thing to note here first, is that Mary accepted Jesus, only to offer him to others. In this way she becomes, for us, an example of what it means to bear witness to Christ and, therefore, to be his missionary in the world. Sometimes we are afraid of the word evangelisation, especially when we try to apply to our own lives of faith. Very often we feel inadequate, and we just do not know what to do, which leads to feelings of being helpless. Yet, Mary makes it very simple. Just be conscious of the fact that wherever you go, you are, in fact, taking Jesus with you. In many ways this is the very meaning of faith. You see sometimes we do not need words but simply to offer Jesus to others through our lives of faith. This is the way of Mary, and she invites it to be our way too.

I have mentioned before, in these reflections, that Pope Francis has often said that Christianity is meant to be a faith of joy. Such joy, in fact, begins with Jesus, and if we have faith in him, if we place all our hope and trust in him, then such joy must find expression in the way in which we live. When Mary rushes to greet Elizabeth, her heart abounds with great joy. Going back to that young woman, in Nazareth, when the angel first appeared to her, the greeting was, *'Rejoice highly favoured one, the Lord is with you.'* In that moment everything changed. Mary's whole life now, would be as the God bearer. She would offer, her son Jesus to the world, and this would be her, Good News. Hence, her heart would be full of joy. There would be pain, suffering and much heartache ahead, but nothing could change the truth of the joy she now felt. The model Mary offers us here, though, is one of service based on love. She listened to God, accepted his invitation, rejoiced, and took Jesus to others, offering the world her Son. On this Fourth Sunday of Advent, as we prepare to celebrate the birth of Jesus again, we would do well to follow the example of Mary. To listen to what God is saying to us, accept his invitation to serve him, place all our hope and trust in him, rejoice, and finally to take Jesus with us, wherever we go, and through our lives of faith, offer him to others.

*Something to think about or discuss:*

1. *Spend a moment or two thinking about the role of women in the life of the church. What conclusions do you come to?*

2. *Reflect on the role of Mary in your own life of faith. How would you describe her role?*

3. *Write down the three most important things you have learnt about Mary from this reflection. Do any of them surprise you?*

4. *What does evangelisation mean? How can you apply it to your own life?*

5. *Do you feel more prepared to celebrate Christmas now? Can you give reasons for your answer?*

# Luke and Christmas

When it comes to Christmas day we always begin with the prologue to John's Gospel. The reason for this is very simple, it explains to us the real meaning of Christmas. John also reveals to us what God is like when he states, '*The Word became flesh and dwelt among us.*' Sadly, however, the commercial world has sort to exploit this to its own financial advantage by distorting the real message Christmas has to offer. However, it is done in a very subtle way by pulling at our heart strings and exploiting our emotions. Yet there, beneath the surface of everything if we take the time to look, waits God. You see although Christmas, for many people at least, makes us feel good, there is always something missing. Something, which we cannot quite put our finger on but has the feeling of making us desire that which we cannot see. This thirst for something other than which we are fed by the commercial world, and those just seeking to have a good time, is our hearts desire for God because, ultimately, only he can satisfy our deepest needs. It is for this reason, that we begin the Christmas season with the prologue to John's Gospel because it makes abundantly clear the fact that it is God who comes in search of us, and he does this for no other reason, than he loves us.

The Holy Family serves to remind us of something which we can easily forget but which is tremendously important if we are to understand something fundamental to our faith. God invites us to call him '*Abba,*' which is a very informal term for father akin to that of dad or daddy. Can you imagine relating to God in that way? Yet this is what he wants us to do, and we are in good company here because this was exactly the same way Jesus referred to his Father. You see if God is our Father does this not mean that we are all brothers and sisters? And what are brothers and sisters invited to do? Exactly! Love each other.

The star that the Magi followed is something that we all have to do, and it is called the journey of faith. Sometimes, like them, we lose our way, but the star still shines inviting us ever forward. To do this, we need to keep our eyes and ears open, always on the lookout, but never giving up. Until we reach that moment in our lives, when we realise, it is not enough just to follow the star, but we must become its light for others. That light is the light of faith, and its source is Jesus Christ himself.

Talking about our journey of faith, sometimes we will meet along the way, the honest enquirer who will ask us what God is like. Our answer will always be the same and just like John the Baptist we must point to Jesus. Sometimes this may involve words but as the well-known saying goes, actions speak much louder. I wonder how my actions this year will reveal Christ to others.

As the Christmas season draws to an end, we will spend some time reflecting on the Holy Spirit and its role in our lives of faith. It is one of those areas that we seem to know very little about, and yet we are both consumed and overwhelmed by it. Perhaps, this gives us a clue as to why it is so neglected, we simply take it for granted. Without the Holy Spirit, we can do nothing. It is the Holy Spirt which leads us to Jesus who, in turn, leads us to the Father. It is the Holy Spirt who invites us to pray and to love and to serve others. Indeed, it was the Holy Spirit that inspired me to write this book. So, although a mystery, the Holy Spirit is God's way of being with us now and always. Why not spend some time, this year, reflecting on the role of the Holy Spirit in your life and what God might just be inviting you to do? When the Apostles did this at Pentecost it changed their lives for ever. Dare we do the same?

**Five:**

## 'The Most Wonderful Time of the Year'

John 1:1-18

### Christmas Day

*In the beginning was the Word, and the Word was with God, and the Word was God. He was in the beginning with God. All things came into being through him, and without him not one thing came into being. What has come into being in him was life, and the life was the light of all people. The light shines in the darkness, and the darkness did not overcome it.*

*There was a man sent from God, whose name was John. He came as a witness to testify to the light, so that all might believe through him. He himself was not the light, but he came to testify to the light. The true light, which enlightens everyone, was coming into the world.*

*He was in the world, and the world came into being through him; yet the world did not know him. He came to what was his own, and his own people did not accept him. But to all who received him, who believed in his name, he gave power to become children of God, who were born, not of blood or of the will of the flesh or of the will of man, but of God.*

*And the Word became flesh and lived among us, and we have seen his glory, the glory as of a father's only son, full of grace and truth. (John testified to him and cried out, "This was he of whom I said, 'He who comes after me ranks ahead of me because he was before me.'") From his fullness we have all received, grace upon grace. The law indeed was given through Moses; grace and truth came through Jesus Christ. No one has ever seen God. It is God the only Son, who is close to the Father's heart, who has made him known.*

I have taken the title for this reflection from that well known Christmas song, *'It's the most wonderful time of the year,'* sung by Andy Williams. I have done this because it raises so many questions such as, why is it the most wonderful time of the year? What do we really celebrate at Christmas? What are we looking for and what do we really want? Is there a link between how we live our lives and what our deepest desires are? Saint Augustine once said, *'Our heart is restless until it rests in you.'* This, I think, points us in the right direction, providing much food for thought. So, let us reflect, for a moment, on what the celebration of Christmas draws both our minds and our hearts to:

- Peace
- Happiness
- Gifts
- Children
- The birth of a child
- Family
- Belonging
- Community

Now let us look at ourselves, and ask what our deepest needs and desires are:

- To be at peace
- To be truly happy
- To belong
- To be in relationships of intimacy
- To experience tenderness and gentleness
- To experience *real* love

Could it be, therefore, that the life we find ourselves living bears no resemblance to what we want it to be? Christmas, however, conjures up images of a life worth living and we find ourselves longing for it. For this reason, we need to go back to Saint Augustine and reflect, ever more deeply, on his words, *'Our heart is restless until it rests in you.'* Is there a restlessness to our lives? Here we must be completely honest with ourselves by admitting that no matter how much money we have or how comfortable in life we are, there is still an absence of true peace. Putting it another way, there is a longing in our hearts, for that which feels beyond our reach. Christmas, however, pulls us back in ways that touch our hearts, which at the same time, feels beyond our understanding.

It is here that we need to spend time reflecting on our own experiences of something which is very real, at this time of the year, our feelings. As we gaze, outwardly, at Christmas, bombarded by the commercial world and its urge to tell us that, *'It's the most wonderful time of the year,'* we need to be aware of what is going in inside of us, in the depths of our hearts. Here we discover the possibility that our deepest desires can take us through and beyond the superficiality of what we are being offered to something far better. Hence Christmas, and indeed life, is not about what we can possess, and therefore enjoy now. Rather, it takes us beyond ourselves, to a better place, where life itself takes on a new dimension altogether. At this point, perhaps, we can recognise that we are, in fact, truly free, and not bound to a life which cannot fulfil our deepest needs. Putting it in a completely different way, Christmas reminds us that there is a life beyond this one and values which turn those of the world completely upside down. Without realising it Christmas challenges everything we have, in fact, ever believed in. After all who would have thought it possible that the Son of God could be born poor, in a stable, and placed in a feeding trough used by animals? Spend a moment or two here going back to what we said about John the Baptist, in the wilderness, compared to the Emperor and the High Priest living lives of luxury in their palaces. This is how God acts. So, what might he be saying to us now?

Christmas challenges us to ask what might be called, ultimate questions. However, the difficulty is that we are distracted and are encouraged to become obsessed with ourselves. Think about the overindulgence of eating, the buying of unnecessary gifts, and the need to focus exclusively on ourselves and our own families. Think further about the stress, worry and anxiety all of this brings, especially to those experiencing financial difficulties. Then think about whether the commercial world cares about any of this or not. All of this serves to do one thing, which is to close our minds and harden our hearts to the bigger issues. God invites us to look to the infinite, which lives deep within our souls. The world on the other hand wants us only to see the superficial and the finite. When we live our lives like that, we become introspective, turning in on ourselves, and without being aware of it begin to lose contact with the divine. Now life is only about what we can feel, touch, taste and see. We have become insensitive to that which is outside of our limited and defined experiences of life. Yet, the God of infinite love waits, and knocks gently on the door of our hearts. The irony is, that part of us knows he is there, and that he is our ultimate destiny, which explains our dissatisfaction with it all.

What then can we do? The answer is a simple one. If you can, take a look at the painting by William Holman Hunt, called, *'Light of the World.'* It depicts Jesus holding a lamp and knocking on a door. If you look closely at the door, it has no handle. The reason for this, is that the door represents our hearts on which Christ knocks. The handle is on the inside and therefore it is up to us to open the door. During the season of Christmas faith invites us both to discover and enter into the mystery of God's great love for us. But we need to do something. The answer lies in a baby, wrapped in swaddling clothes and lying in a manger. It is both simple and wonderful at the same time. The fact is that God has come to find us, simply because he loves us, more than we could ever know. Think back to the image of Christ knocking on the door of our hearts and of the child lying in the manager. This is how close God has come to us and now it is our turn to come to him.

What then does it take on this Christmas day to recognise just how close God, through his Son, is to us? The first thing we need to do, is wake up to the fact, that God is here with us now. This God comes to us in a way the world did not expect, through a small child lying in a manger. It is like God crept in through the back door whilst the world was looking the other way. We must find him in the same way. The first step, is to open our hearts by recognising that the restlessness we know lies deep within each of us, can only be satisfied by God. The second thing we need to do, is to let go of everything we know we do not need, which prevents us from approaching this child. Then quietly, and gently, with hearts open wide we can discover a truth, in that manger, which has always been there. That God, in fact, is closer to us than we could ever imagine and loves us more than we could ever know. In that moment we can also discover, perhaps, for the first time, the real meaning of Christmas, and that our lives have already been transformed, and will never be the same again. The key to everything, however, is our willingness to open our hearts to God, holding, literally, nothing back, in the same way that God, through the sending of his Son, opened his heart to us.

*Something to think about or discuss:*

    *1. What does Christmas mean to you?*

    *2. In the eyes of the world, what has Christmas become?*

    *3. How would you describe the real meaning of Christmas?*

    *4. What does the birth of Jesus say to the world of today?*

    *5. In what ways does Christmas challenge us?*

# Six:

## 'The Family of Humanity'

Luke 2:41-52

## The Holy Family

*Now every year his parents went to Jerusalem for the festival of the Passover. And when he was twelve years old, they went up as usual for the festival. When the festival was ended and they started to return, the boy Jesus stayed behind in Jerusalem, but his parents did not know it. Assuming that he was in the group of travellers, they went a day's journey. Then they started to look for him among their relatives and friends. When they did not find him, they returned to Jerusalem to search for him. After three days they found him in the temple, sitting among the teachers, listening to them, and asking them questions. And all who heard him were amazed at his understanding and his answers. When his parents saw him, they were astonished; and his mother said to him, "Child, why have you treated us like this? Look, your father and I have been searching for you in great anxiety." He said to them, "Why were you searching for me? Did you not know that I must be in my Father's house?" But they did not understand what he said to them. Then he went down with them and came to Nazareth and was obedient to them. His mother treasured all these things in her heart.*

There are a number of different ways we could celebrate and reflect upon the Holy Family. The traditional way is to use the model of Nazareth, with Jesus, Mary, and Joseph as the example for all Christian families to follow. We could then go on to talk about the importance of the family unit in the world today. Here we are using the Holy Family as the ideal to which we should all aspire. Yet, perhaps, this year, we should try to do something different. Remembering how radical Jesus was let us now reflect on something, which was dear to his own heart, and present throughout the whole of his earthly ministry. Here I am, in fact, referring to each other, and our membership of the universal human race. Just think about the opening words of the Lord's Prayer, *'Our Father.'* Does this not declare, right from the start, that if God is our Father, then we must all be brothers and sisters to each other, and in that sense, part of one big family? Indeed, this was something Jesus's own family had to learn for themselves as they strove to understand his mission.

In the Gospel reading for today, we find Mary and Joseph, out of their minds with worry, as they struggle to find the missing Jesus. Where he is, they do not know. We can only imagine what both of them were going through as they searched everywhere to find him. It begs the question, why would Jesus do this to them? Did he intend to cause them heartache? Could he not have told them what he intended to do or maybe even asked their permission? It is for all these reasons and, perhaps, more that Mary on finding Jesus, offers him a piece of her mind, *'My son, why have you treated us like this? Your father and I have been anxiously looking for you.'* The response of Jesus is both intriguing and mystifying as it becomes clear that his parents do not understand what is going on at all, *'Why were you searching for me? Didn't you know I had to be in my Father's house?'*

Many years later, Jesus will be teaching the crowds when we are told that his mother and his brothers turn up wanting to speak to him. Jesus responds to this request by asking, *'Who is my mother? Who are my bothers? And stretching out his hand towards his disciples he said, 'Here are my mother and my brothers, for whoever does the will of my Father in heaven is my brother and sister and mother.'* Here we see a universal and inclusive Jesus who includes everyone and excludes no one from his family. This serves to provide us with a real insight into Jesus and therefore how God sees us.

What then can we learn from all of this that we can apply in our own lives of faith today? Firstly, that we need to be more like Jesus, by having an inclusive attitude when it comes to other people, and by seeing everyone as part of the one human family. This, in turn, will then affect how we treat and look after one another because we are now, at least attempting, to live our lives as God intended. In this way the church, society and our families will become more caring and understanding as we recognise and accept responsibility for each other.

At this point we can now see the celebration of the Holy Family as a direct challenge as to how we are living out our lives of faith today. Thus, are we committed to helping shape the kind of society and world, which is a true reflection of what Jesus actually taught, and lived? Are we committed to the needs of each other, seeking to relieve the pain, misery and suffering of others, even those we do not know and are, for want of a better way of saying it, not like us? Are we committed to building a world of justice, fairness, and equality for all people? Do we seek the way of mercy, compassion, forgiveness, and love when it comes to all our neighbours? Are we really committed to a world which strives to ensure peace for all people? If any of this rings true then it must begin somewhere, and perhaps that place is within our own homes and parishes.

The source for everything is Jesus because without him none of this makes sense. Hence, we need to return to him as the core and heart of our lives. Growing in our love for Christ is everything because out of our love for him, will pour forth our love for each other. This then must be the starting point for our revolution. Our homes, families, parishes, and schools must rediscover an enthusiasm for Jesus. We must bathe and warm ourselves in his love to the point that our whole being is transformed by it, and we feel compelled to build a world built on the rock of faith. Here the church must point to and lead the way, by being a light to the nations and the source of all hope and truth for a humanity in danger of losing its very soul to the increasing rise in rampant commercialism and individualism. For this reason, the church, as the body of Christ on earth, must seek to include everyone and exclude no one, just as Jesus did. Only by doing this can the church claim to be an authentic witness to its Lord and Master. As we are drawn, ever deeper, into this understanding of the vision Jesus had for humanity, then not only do we become more like him, but more human too,

So, when you pray, say, 'Our Father .........'

*Something to read about or discuss:*

1. *Why is today's celebration important and what does it mean to you?*

2. *What is the most important lesson we can learn from today's reading? Can you give reasons for your answer?*

3. *In your opinion is the church today more inclusive than it was in years gone by.*

4. *In what way, if any, is the church exclusive? That is, in your opinion, does it in any way, exclude people? Can you think of specific examples?*

5. *Thinking about today's reading and reflection, what kind of church do you want to belong to? Are there things, you believe, the church should be doing, to be more inclusive?*

**Seven:**

**'Follow that Star'**

Matthew 2:1-12

## The Epiphany

*In the time of King Herod, after Jesus was born in Bethlehem of Judea, wise men from the East came to Jerusalem, asking, "Where is the child who has been born king of the Jews? For we observed his star at its rising and have come to pay him homage." When King Herod heard this, he was frightened, and all Jerusalem with him; and calling together all the chief priests and scribes of the people, he inquired of them where the Messiah was to be born. They told him, "In Bethlehem of Judea; for so it has been written by the prophet: 'And you, Bethlehem, in the land of Judah, are by no means least among the rulers of Judah; for from you shall come a ruler who is to shepherd my people, Israel.'"*

*Then Herod secretly called for the wise men and learned from them the exact time when the star had appeared. Then he sent them to Bethlehem, saying, "Go and search diligently for the child; and when you have found him, bring me word so that I may also go and pay him homage." When they had heard the king, they set out; and there, ahead of them, went the star that they had seen at its rising, until it stopped over the place where the child was. When they saw that the star had stopped, they were overwhelmed with joy. On entering the house, they saw the child with Mary his mother; and they knelt down and paid him homage. Then, opening their treasure chests, they offered him gifts of gold, frankincense, and myrrh. And having been warned in a dream not to return to Herod, they left for their own country by another road.*

When I think of the Magi following that star, I often find myself taking comfort from the fact that, at times, they were lost and found themselves surrounded by complete darkness. The star, of course, was still there, it was just that, for a while at least, they could not see it. Our lives of faith can often be like that, in so far as, we look for the light but sometimes, it is just so hard to find. Indeed, on occasion, the darkness threatens to overwhelm us. Here I often find myself being drawn to the words of the prophet Isaiah, *The people walking in darkness have seen a great light. On those living in the land of the shadow of death a light has dawned.'* And how we all need that light now. Our faith invites us to constantly look for the light when others see only darkness. From time-to-time people say to me, surely it is easy to believe in God. My response to this is always the same, which is that, in my opinion, it is far easier not to believe in God because that means we are not required to do anything. Whereas believing in God always requires us to act because doing nothing is never an option.

Hence, as followers of Christ today, we are always invited to seek the light even when everyone else sees only darkness. It is for this reason, that the church is called to be a light to the nations and the source of hope and truth for all people. Sometimes, as we know, that light is hard to find but it is always there shining in the darkness. Jesus knew this all too well and perhaps it was for this reason he referred to himself as, *'The Light of the world.'* He also invited those who followed him to be like a lamp placed on a stand, shining for others to see. Hence, there is a constant message here not only to seek and follow the light but, in our lives, to reflect it, whilst recognising that it is Christ himself who is the source.

Going back to the Magi we can now learn something further from their example. They came from the east and journeyed a long way following that tiny light in the sky. At times they lost their way, but they kept going knowing that the light was still there. This, in turn for us, is what faith is like. It invites us to believe and trust in God, even when it feels we are surrounded by darkness, the light still shines. Our problem, however, can very often arise from the fact that we live in times when it has become far easier to see and give in to the darkness. This, in turn, can give rise to feelings of helplessness and despair when people just cannot see any hope in the midst of human tragedy. Yet, Christians by virtue of their faith in Christ, are always called to bear witness to the kind of hope, which in truth, only God can offer. It is for this reason, that human history always teaches us an important lesson. That no matter how much progress we think we are making there will always be a darkness, which accompanies it. There are those, for example, who have and continue to argue that we do not need God. Yet without his light, where would we be?

There is something within us which always seeks the light, a desperate need to find hope rather than succumbing to the darkness. This again is what the Magi teaches us as they journeyed ever forward, always seeking, never looking back, knowing, believing, and trusting that the light would lead them, ultimately, to the truth. At Christmas we learn that it is God, in fact, who came to seek us out first, and that he is closer to jus than we could ever imagine and loves us more than we could ever know. It is for this reason, we believe, that the darkness can never consume us and that there will always be hope because God will never abandon or leave us. Christians can, therefore, be a force for goodness in the world, yet only because we recognise that the source of the light can only be found in a child lying in a manger.

The Magi journeyed long and far experiencing moments of darkness whereby they might well have been tempted to give up and return home. However, the pull of the star was greater than any of this because it would lead them to their real home and their final destiny, God himself. Here we learn, once again, that all things are possible with God. The Magi overcame every adversity, obstacle, and period of darkness in their journey to find the Christ child. In him they found the light of the world, a light more powerful than any darkness, which would, in the course of time, transform everything. For this reason, we can live our lives in the sure and certain hope that no matter how much darkness surrounds us the light to which we look, that of Christ himself, will overcome all things. One day the darkness will cease, and when that happens, we will know, only light.

*Something to think about or discuss:*

1. *Do you think it is easier to believe or not believe in God? Can you explain why?*

2. *Can you think of examples of darkness in the world today?*

3. *What can we learn from the journey of the Magi which may help us live our lives of faith more effectively?*

4. *How important do you think it is for Christians to be people of hope?*

5. *Can you draw any comparisons between the story of the Magi and the role of the church in the world today?*

# Eight:

## 'This is What God is Like'

John 1:1-18

## Second Sunday after Christmas

*In the beginning was the Word, and the Word was with God, and the Word was God. He was in the beginning with God. All things came into being through him, and without him not one thing came into being. What has come into being in him was life, and the life was the light of all people. The light shines in the darkness, and the darkness did not overcome it.*

*There was a man sent from God, whose name was John. He came as a witness to testify to the light, so that all might believe through him. He himself was not the light, but he came to testify to the light. The true light, which enlightens everyone, was coming into the world.*

*He was in the world, and the world came into being through him; yet the world did not know him. He came to what was his own, and his own people did not accept him. But to all who received him, who believed in his name, he gave power to become children of God, who were born, not of blood or of the will of the flesh or of the will of man, but of God.*

*And the Word became flesh and lived among us, and we have seen his glory, the glory as of a father's only son, full of grace and truth. (John testified to him and cried out, "This was he of whom I said, 'He who comes after me ranks ahead of me because he was before me.'") From his fullness we have all received, grace upon grace. The law indeed was given through Moses; grace and truth came through Jesus Christ. No one has ever seen God. It is God the only Son, who is close to the Father's heart, who has made him known.*

If someone were to ask you to describe God, what would you say and where would you begin? Spend a few moments thinking about this before giving some thought to the fact that, according to scripture, no one has, in fact, ever seen God. So, how can we describe that, which we have not seen? These days we need only spend, literally, seconds trawling the internet to find, so called, images of God. Then again, if we were brought up as Christians, we would have been bombarded with other people telling us what

God is like. I know this to be true myself having spent many years, in front of young people, in the classroom. So, what are we to do when other people turn to us and ask, *what is God like?*

Think of it like this. How is it possible to describe the perfection of God? How is possible to say anything about the mystery of God. How is possible to say anything about God who is completely beyond anything we have ever experienced? How is it possible to say anything about God who is other than that which we are? Indeed, anything we attempt to say about God must, on the basis of what we have said so far, be fundamentally flawed. Given that our efforts will always fall short, the danger is that we will always provide our enquirer with our own perception of God, which in truth, may well be wrong to say the least. At this point we may well be tempted to stop or give up, but there is no need for such a defeatist attitude, just as long as we can admit to ourselves that we do not have all the answers. This is because, at the end of the day, we are all in the same boat.

So let me repeat again, no one has ever seen God. This includes popes, priests, theologians, bishops, and teachers, as well as you and me. So we are, in fact, in good company. Indeed, there is a danger, in so called experts claiming they know all there is to know about God, and we must, if truth be told, guard against this. Why? Because as I keep on saying, no one has ever seen God. At this point we may well also ask, are we any nearer to knowing and understanding what God is like. Well, the answer to this question is, perhaps, closer than you might expect.

Go back and have a read at the prologue to John's Gospel given at the start of this reflection and see if you notice anything. Well? The answer is, of course, Jesus. I remember telling my students, on a number of occasions, that the answer to every question ever asked is, Jesus. This, I must admit, really confused them but let me now, take a moment or two, to explain why I gave them this answer. The very last sentence of the prologue to John's Gospel reads like this, *'No one has ever seen God; it is the only begotten Son, who is close to the Father's heart, who has made him known.'* Or putting it another way Jesus, and Jesus alone, reveals to us what God, in fact, is like.

Now we can move on to our next question, how does Jesus show us what God is like then? Once again John, in his Gospel tells, us, *'The Word became flesh and lived among us.'* In other words, God became like us, in his Son, to show us exactly what he is like, and we call this the incarnation. Indeed, this is exactly what we celebrated at Christmas and continue to celebrate today. This is a marvellous and liberating thing because, in essence, it means that we do not need long complex, and detailed theology books, as important as they may be, but only Jesus Christ, if we are to know anything about God. So, if you want to know what God is like, then the simple message is, look to Jesus. And if you want to drawer closer to God, then in the same way, draw closer to Jesus. Hence the more you know about Jesus the more you will know about God and equally the more you fall in love with Jesus then the more you will fall in love with God. As a result, when people say to me, and they do, *'I do not believe in God!'* I always ask, *'have you read the Gospels?'* Spend any time, at all, with the Gospels and you are, in fact, spending time with God, because they tell us all about the life, death and resurrection of Jesus, who is God made flesh.

Yet, the reverse of this process is also true. The further we move away from Jesus then the further we are moving away from God. It is for this reason, that I like quoting Saint Augustine of Hippo who put it like this, *'The further we move away from the light the darker and colder it gets.'* Now go back to the prologue in John's Gospel where we find, *'The true light, that gives light to everyone was coming into the world.'* Later in the same Gospel Jesus was also to refer to himself as, *'The light of the world.'* This means there can be no substitute for Jesus if we are to know anything about God at all. It is for this reason that Jesus needs to be at the very heart of our lives, our homes, our parishes, and our schools. Only then can we claim to know anything about God.

Doctrines, theology, tradition, rules, and regulations may all be important, but you cannot fall in love with any of them. Indeed, unless they lead us to Jesus how important are they? The simple truth is, that the closer we live our lives to Jesus, the more we become aware of his overwhelming, and unconditional love for us. The result of this is reciprocal, in so far as, our response is to love him, and in turn each other, in the same way. It is here we also learn something of the Holy Trinity too, because our hearts are pierced by the Holy Spirt poured into them, overflowing from the love which exists between the Father and Son. It is this Holy Spirit, which leads us to the Son, Jesus, who, in turn, leads us to the Father. In this way our lives give expression to the Trinity as we make known Father and Son through living lives of faith.

Ultimately, any goodness which we manifest in our lives is simply a pale reflection of the goodness of God. Yet, it remains that, something of God. We can only do this because of our closeness to Jesus and we can get ever closer to him through the Gospels. As we start a New Year together, I would urge you to return to the Gospels, and through them deepen your relationship with Christ. This year we are in Year C, so our Gospel is that of Luke, which is sometimes described as the Gospel of the poor. At the beginning of this reflection, I asked you to describe what God is like, I wonder how you would answer this question now.

Jesus urged us, *'To love God with all our heart, soul, body, and mind and to love our neighbours as ourselves.'* This year why not focus some of your time loving Jesus more and see what happens to your life of faith. John tells us, *'The Word was made flesh and lived among us,'* closer to us than we could ever imagine and loving us more than we could ever know. For some reason I never grow tired of saying this because for me, and I hope for you, the reader, it happens to be true.

*Something to think about or discuss:*

1. *How would you describe what God is like to the honest enquirer?*

2. *How is it possible to know anything about God?*

3. *What does the prologue to John's Gospel tell us about God?*

4. *Why is Jesus so important to our lives of faith?*

5. *How can this New Year be different when it comes to developing our relationship with God? Explain, if you can, why this is important.*

# Nine:

## 'Rediscovering the Holy Spirit'

Luke 3:15-16, 21-22

## The Baptism of the Lord

*As the people were filled with expectation, and all were questioning in their hearts concerning John, whether he might be the Messiah, John answered all of them by saying, "I baptize you with water; but one who is more powerful than I is coming; I am not worthy to untie the thong of his sandals. He will baptize you with the Holy Spirit and fire.*

*Now when all the people were baptized, and when Jesus also had been baptized and was praying, the heaven was opened, and the Holy Spirit descended upon him in bodily form like a dove. And a voice came from heaven, "You are my Son, the Beloved; with you I am well pleased."*

It has been my experience that many Christians are not quite sure what to make of the Holy Spirit, which features so prominently in our reading for today, as we celebrate the baptism of Jesus. Listen again to what John the Baptist has to say, *'I baptise you with water. But one more powerful than I am will come, the thongs of whose sandals I am not worthy to untie. He will baptise you with the Holy Spirit and with fire.'* At this point, let me take you to the room where the disciples waited for the first coming of the Holy Spirit ten days after the Ascension. Once again Luke, this time in the Acts of the Apostles, describes the Holy Spirit in terms of wind and fire, which transformed the apostles into evangelisers not caring whether they lived or died. The only thing they knew, was that they had to bear witness to Jesus. It is this same Holy Spirit which is as present to us today. as it was for the Apostles, over two thousand years ago.

When people still, however, get stuck on what the Holy Spirit is I go back to something I reflected on earlier. When Jesus returned to the Father, taking our humanity with him, such was the overwhelming, and unconditional love they had for each other, it could not be contained. Hence, it over-spilled or poured out of their hearts into ours and continues to do so, even now. We experience the Holy Spirit in a special way through the sacraments but most obviously when we are baptised and confirmed. Let us recall that when we are baptised it is Christ himself who baptises us, not only sharing his eternal life with us, but equally making us part of his body on earth, the church. Later, and most often, when we are old enough to appreciate what is going on, the sacrament of confirmation seals the gift of the Holy Spirit in our souls. This means that the Holy Spirit is, and always will be, alive and active in our lives. The problem is that we often fail to recognise it.

Going back to our reading for today, the early Christians saw themselves as being totally reliant on the Holy Spirit. Indeed, it was the Holy Spirit which energised them and bound them together as a community of faith. This brought with it a challenge for them, which applies equally to us – the invitation to live our lives in a new and completely different way. You see the Holy Spirit allows us to experience God. Remember what we said about how it is constantly being poured out directly from the Farther and the Son into our hearts? In this way the Holy Spirit leads us to Jesus and Jesus leads us to the Father, which makes it possible for us, here and now, to share directly in the life of God. This in turn, has the effect of defining who we are as individuals as well communities of faith.

Going on further from this, the Holy Spirit also sets us free to live our lives in communion with both God and each other. This then, in turn, is reflected by the way in which we live our lives according to the law of love. Here mercy, compassion, justice, forgiveness, peace, and reconciliation spring forth from everything we do because our lives have been animated by the Holy Spirit. The effect of this, is that it defines our communities, which become examples to society, of what life could be like.

If this can be achieved, then something else can also be discovered which is, that it is possible to reflect how we live our lives of faith through how we worship. Without realising it the Holy Spirit already dominates what we do in church, enabling bread to become body and wine to become blood, inviting us to pray and hear what God is saying to us through his Word. Yet the whole ritual of worship needs to be animated by the Spirit, bringing joy to our hearts and minds as we worship God, in Christ, together.

Only the Holy Spirit, therefore, can transform our lives, enabling us to live as authentic witnesses to Christ. It is for this reason that we constantly need to turn to the Holy Spirit asking for the strength to prevail in our journey of faith. Thomas Merton made the point that God will never refuse us the gift of his Spirit. Yet, what is also true is that we need to accept it, and see it for what it really is, God's gift of himself to us. On the day we realise and accept this, our lives will change, and will never be the same again.

*Something to think about or discuss:*

1. *What does the Holy Spirit mean to you?*

2. *How would you explain the role of the Holy Spirit, in your life of faith, to someone else?*

3. *Why do you think the Holy Spirit is very often described as flames or fire?*

4. *Has the church, in your opinion, neglected to teach people successfully about the Holy Spirit and how it works?*

5. *How is the Holy Spirit visible in the life of the church today?*

# Who Stole Christmas?
# Some Final Thoughts

As I write this final part of the book, I find myself reflecting on the way in which society appears to be on a slippery slope, sliding further and further away from the real meaning of Christmas. After all, if you take Jesus out of Christmas, what is really left? This, I think, is the crux of the problem because if Jesus is removed from Christmas, where is the challenge, where is the meaning and where is the true source of everything? So, is there really then, an agenda to remove Jesus from Christmas and if so, why?

I can only answer this question from my own point of view, and in the spirit of what I have already written in the previous pages. Yet, I maintain, that even in those who deny the existence of Jesus, whilst celebrating Christmas, something of him and his presence still remains. You see, God, as we have already said, comes in search of us, even though we might reject him, because he loves us. Or putting it another way, God's love for us, expressed through his Son, is not conditional on us believing in him. That is what makes his love so difficult to grasp for many people. If this is true, however, then God is closer to all of us than any of us could ever imagine and loves us more than any of us could ever know.

It is for this reason that I maintain, the closeness of God to us, through his Son, touches our very souls and opens our hearts, and this is what many people experience, albeit, unknowingly, at Christmas. The great sadness to this, however, is that the vast majority of people are totally unaware of it. The fact that God, himself, is bound up in our humanity. As a result, many people do not see the God who Jesus came to reveal, the one born poor, in a stable and placed in a manger. The one who throughout his earthly life, went deliberately, in search of the despised, rejected, unwanted and unloved. The God who yearns for us to be free and to love each other in the same way he loves us. The God who welcomes all people and turns no one way. In many ways, this makes us feel uncomfortable, but it is meant to because it raises fundamental questions about society and how we look after the weak and the vulnerable. Perhaps, this is another reason to take Jesus out of Christmas as he confronts us with what it means to put his teaching into practice. In which case, it is far easier to decorate our trees, wrap up our presents, gorge ourselves on food, and enjoy our festive-filled parties, whilst, at the same time, turning a blind eye to those in need.

Hence, my primary intention in writing this book, is to put Jesus back into the heart of Christmas, and help as many people as possible, realise this truth. I am fully aware of the fact that, perhaps, many of the people I am writing this book for will never read it. However, this is where, you, the reader, comes in. If you have taken the time to work your way through the pages of this book, you might find yourself now, even in part, agreeing with me. If you do, then why not join with me in doing something? In this way this book becomes a catalyst for action, and anything is possible. I said earlier that the call to discipleship is an invitation to action because doing nothing is never an option when we follow Jesus. Hence the fundamental question is, how can we help people realise the constant presence of Christ in their lives, now? Yet, the starting point for this must be with us because we must live it and believe it first. My hope is that this book has gone someway in deepening your faith, which might just lead you to something else.

Once we realise, that the Christmas story is a revelation, telling us that our lives are bound to that of God himself, then everything changes. For now, we realise and understand, that we do not have to rely on our own strength, but on his, to cope with the daily struggles of life. In this way our lives can be filled with a renewed hope for the future, knowing that wherever we go, and whatever we do, God-is-with-us. And this is something that others must see when they look at us, and the church, to which we belong.

Perhaps, many people, in recent years, have left the church because they no longer feel the presence of Jesus there. Well, if this is the case, then it is up to us to do something about it. But this will only happen when we build our lives on the rock of our faith, Jesus Christ. At Christmas when God came in search of us, and became one-with-us, everything changed. It is now time for us to be that change.

Finally, you will have noticed and perhaps shared in, the questions I have placed at the end of each reflection. As you have finished this book, why not now, write down some questions of your own. Or better still, why not write down five things you intend to do now as a result of reading this book and then see what happens.

God Bless.

Deacon Sean
*October 13th, 2023*

# About the Author

Sean Loone is a Roman Catholic Deacon working in the Archdiocese of Birmingham. He has spent much of his career teaching in a variety of schools and colleges combining this with lecturing part-time at Saint Mary's College Oscott, the seminary for the Archdiocese. Currently he acts as chaplain and Religious Education advisor to a number of academic establishments including Our Lady of the Wayside, his home parish, where he is also the Catholic Life governor. His academic interests, on which he has published many articles, include Biblical studies and Christology. His most recent publication was a book called, **'Words of Life – The Parables of Jesus for People Today'**. He also has extensive pastoral and sacramental experience combining this with a ministry dedicated to proclaiming God's word through both preaching and teaching the scriptures. He is married with three sons and is currently working on a new project, which aims, this time, to explore finding Christ in the Sunday Gospels of Lent and Easter.

# By the Same Author

*'Born for Us*
*— A Journey into the Real Meaning of Christmas'*

Available from ALIVE Publishing (2019)


*'Only in the Crucified Christ*
*— Questions and Answers on Faith, Hope and Love'*

Available from Amazon (2020)
All profits to CAFOD


*'Sharing in the Life of God*
*— A Journey into the Real Meaning of Easter'*

Available from Amazon (2021)
All profits to the Father O'Mahony Memorial Trust


*'Servants of the Word*
*— The Gospel of Christ and the Call to Discipleship'*

Available from Amazon (2021)
All profits to Father Hudson's Care


*'Words of Life*
*— The Parables of Jesus for People Today'*

Michael Terence Publishing (2022)
All Profits to CAFOD

# Thank You

In writing this book, for me at least, it is inevitable to conclude, that some of it, if not all of it, is an expression of my own faith. It is for this reason that I now need to recognise, in this *'thank you,'* some of those people who have helped me along the way. You see faith, in many ways, often, does not just happen, although it is important for me to concede that sometimes it does just that. Here though, I want to pay tribute to the people who came before me, whose faith led the way, and on whose shoulders I now stand. It is most humbling for me now to go back to my roots and the country of my origin, Ireland. It was there that my late grandmother, Kate Conroy, lived in the county of Mayo (Maigh Eo). Her life was hard, harsh, and ravaged by poverty, and yet she still kept the faith. Indeed, faith to her was as natural as the air that she breathed. Alongside her, I place my own mother Bridget or Bridie as many people called her. This is not the place to go into the many beatings life gave her, but by living through it she taught me more about the faith than I have learnt from any book. It was from these two great women that I learned the true meaning of faith, and this book is a reflection of that. The great challenge for the believer is not only to find Christ in the Gospels but also in life itself, even though, at times, it can be very cruel. So, in conclusion, and in these my final words in this book, I thank not only Kate and Bridget Conroy but the people of Mayo and the land of Ireland to whom I owe so much.

God Bless.

Deacon Sean

*'The promise that was made is for you and your children,*
*and for all those who are far away,*
*for all whom the Lord our God is calling to himself.'*

*(Acts of the Apostles 2:39)*


*'For I am certain of this: neither death nor life, no angels,*
*nor principalities, nothing already in existence*
*and nothing still to come, nor any power,*
*nor the heights nor the depths,*
*nor any created thing whatever. Will be able to come*
*between us and the love of God, known to us in Christ Jesus*
*our Lord.'*

*(Romans 8:38-39)*


*'Do not be afraid. Look, I bring you news of great joy,*
*a joy to be shared by the whole people. Today in the town of*
*David a Saviour has been born to you; he is Christ the Lord.*
*And here is sign for you: you will find a baby*
*wrapped in swaddling clothes and lying in a manger.'*

*(Luke 2:10-13)*


*'Heaven and earth will pass away,*
*but my words will never pass away.'*

*(Matthew 24:35)*

*Available worldwide from Amazon*

---

Michael Terence
Publishing

www.mtp.agency

www.facebook.com/mtp.agency

@mtp_agency

Printed in Great Britain
by Amazon

28519856R00081